THE HEALTHY STUDENT COOKBOOK

from

First published in Great Britain in 2016
by Orion Publishing Group Ltd
Carmelite House, 50 Victoria Embankment
London EC4Y 0DZ
An Hachette UK Company

10 9 8 7 6 5 4 3 2 1

A CIP catalogue record for this book is available from the British Library.

ISBN: 978 0 2978 7000 5

Words and recipes: Rob Allison
Photography: Andrew Hayes-Watkins

Designed by Bryony Clark
Printed and bound by CPI Group (UK) Ltd, Croydon CR0 4YY

The Orion Publishing Group's policy is to use papers that are natural,
renewable and recyclable products and made from wood grown in sustainable
forests. The logging and manufacturing processes are expected to conform to
the environmental regulations of the country of origin.

www.orionbooks.co.uk

While every effort ha[s] been made [to...] of the information
in this book is correc[t...] for nutritional
advice from a medica[l] pro[...]

Contents

Lunch 35

Dinner

Sides & Snacks 163

Desserts & Treats 185

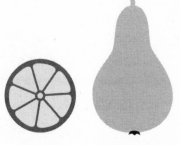

Introduction:
the modern student

As Bob Dylan prophesied way back when, 'the times they are a-changin''. Whilst he may have been talking geopolitically, we are talking about something far more important: student diet. Gone are the greasy beans-on-toast, cheap vodka guzzling hoi polloi, and in-coming are you, the new generation who own NutriBullets, read *Deliciously Ella* and are conscious of looking after yourselves, mind, body and soul.

We at Student Beans applaud this shift: we applaud your self-awareness and the desire to do better than just drink yourself stupid and wait for the 2:2 to roll in. We want to help and as such, this book is written with the modern student in mind.

There are many student cookbooks out there which will tell you how to eat well on a budget, how to cook scrambled eggs in the microwave and how to prepare minced beef 150 different ways, but this book will push you a little further into a brave new world of unrefined sugars, whole grains and lactose-free options. True, the students of the past may sneer and wonder what the world has come to when their successors would rather eat quinoa than a greasy kebab, but they can live with their diabetes and liver cirrhosis whilst we breathe and move freely in our non-bloated, Lycra-clad skin.

There are of course other books out there that concentrate on healthy eating and you may already own one or several of them. Those books are good but they aren't specifically written with studentkind in mind. Our recipes are engineered to work within the parameters of student life, be that a lack of funds, a lack of equipment or a simple lack of time and energy. We have your needs at the heart of our ethos.

Eating well doesn't have to cost the earth

Flicking through the technicolour pages of modern, healthy-eating cookery books may set your appetite into overdrive and give you impetus enough to push you out the door in search of life-giving alfalfa and ancient grains of mystic digestive power, but often the excitement of newly discovered healthy ingredients is keenly followed by the stark realisation that whilst kind to your gut, health foods are not so kind to your bank balance.

Spirulina shots, wheatgrass smoothies and Medjool dates do not come cheap; where once they were obscure ingredients found in amongst the aisles of vegan stores, they have become the stalwarts of the high street supermarkets who have taken to the healthy-eating fad like crispy duck to a pancake. If we were cynics, we would suggest that the supermarkets are cashing in on everybody's new-found body conscientiousness and glibly hiking up the prices of popular, healthy ingredients – but we're far too Zen for that level of suspicion. There are, however, ways round the supermarket giants. Here are a few tips to help save the pennies:

Roll up, roll up

Markets, remember them? They generally exist in most major cities and towns and are an excellent place to find cheap fruit and veg. Rock up a little later in the day and listen to the prices tumble as the traders try to flog the remains of their stock. Blueberries, raspberries, apples and kale will all be found in your local market at a much lower price than the supermarkets offer. Find your local market, head down and revel in a refreshingly vibrant shopping experience.

Cornershop cooking

Your local cornershop is not just for last-minute party drinks, they also stock food. We're not talking so much about the salami-filled fridge or the munchie aisles, but about the dried spice and tinned food sections. Oily fish, lentils and spices are not only available at your local cornershop, but we will bet you they are cheaper, and of better quality, than those found in the supermarkets.

Ditch the meat

Removing meat from your diet is not only good for your body and the environment, but it will also drastically reduce your food bill leaving you with a bit more cash to pick up tasty fruit, nuts or grains. We have worked hard to include a lot of recipes in this book that do not contain meat so take advantage of our giving nature.

Go ethnic

Every major city will have at least one ethnic area. Learn to harness the produce found in these areas as they are way cheaper than anything found on the high street and more often than not better quality. You will find an abundance of ingredients such as lentils, gram flour, spices, herbs, and fruit and veg at a fraction of the price the supermarkets are flogging them for.

Herd mentality

If you tried to eat an entire 5kg of lentils over the course of a term you may have saved yourself a fortune in food, but you will have probably spent the saved cash on loo roll. Share out those 5kg of lentils and all of a sudden you and your buddies are richer and healthier – double win. Jokes aside, pooling your monetary resources and then eating together will save you a fortune. Heading down to the market and picking up monster-sized bags of grains and spices is a great way to save money and it also negates all those little, but expensive trips to the shop to pick up last-minute ingredients.

Know your enemy

Sugars

Here at Student Beans we don't like to jump on bandwagons or be swayed too strongly by the ever-changing popular press; we like to take more of an erudite, informed opinion. With those words in mind, we can safely say: sugar is really bad for you. Unlike any other foodstuff, sugar has no positive effect on the body or mind. We know it tastes great and believe us, sugary snacks are often consumed at Student Beans HQ, but it is important to understand that just a small reduction in sugar intake can have an incredibly positive influence on the health of your body.

Very boringly it's all about moderation . . . so dull, we know. Realistically, studentkind is not going to stop scoffing gummy sweets, drinking wine or guzzling cider, but we challenge you not to spoon, sprinkle or scatter any additional sugar on to any product you consume, and to also pay attention to the amount of sugar already hiding within your cereals, ready meals and snacks. We hope that simply being aware of how much sugar there is out there, for a short period of time, will shock you into action. You will find that as you avoid sugar, it will become increasingly easy to carry on. Sugar is addictive, so if you can break the saccharine cycle just for a few days your taste buds will stop craving sweet treats and you will soon find anything overly sweet becomes just that.

To help you along your way, we pledge not to add any refined sugars to any of the recipes in this book. Instead we will use the natural sugars of fruits and honey to sweeten our puds. We are fully aware that naturally occurring fructose is no better for you than refined caster sugar, but nature has a wonderful way of packaging products well. For example, if you eat a date, not only are you taking on the bad sugars, but you will also be eating a huge amount of fibre which we all know is good for our digestive system, and there is also a decent amount of carbohydrate in a date which tempers the release of insulin and reduces the amount of work the liver and pancreas have to do – do not worry if you find any of this too dull or too complicated to follow, we have done the thinking for you.

Whole grains and complex carbs

Even if you only take a passing interest in the world of health foods, we are sure you will have heard these phrases said, but what do they really mean and are they just a fad? Let us explain.

Whole grains are exactly that: grains that haven't been processed and so come as nature intended with the bran, germ and endosperm all still intact. During the refining process which creates products such as plain flour and white rice, the germ and the bran are lost and considering these two parts are the ones enriched with antioxidants and vitamins, what you are left with is pretty much nutrient-poor stodge. Great for cooking with, but not so great for your body.

Whilst not so good for us, refined grains are manna to the food industry as they are less volatile in both their raw and cooked states, leading to a greater shelf life. They also produce a blander product both in terms of taste and texture, which translates to a broader customer appeal. We can totally see why food manufacturers have evolved to stripping back grains, but what is good for them is not so good for us, or more specifically our guts. A bit like 'coming off' sugar, reducing our intake of refined grains is tricky: they are in so many food products that we have grown up with that both our mouths and brains expect them to be present. But we promise you that it only takes a week or two for your tastes to change and then eating brown pasta or wholemeal bread will seem totally natural, and if you return to the processed white bread of the past, it will taste like the playdough it is.

If you start eating whole grains in place of processed ones, you will naturally start eating complex carbs, which is just a fancy way of saying carbs that take longer to digest. The benefit of these types of carbs is that they release their energy over a much longer period of time, which gives you a longer lasting boost of energy. The opposite happens when you eat processed carbs: they are very quickly broken down into sugars by the body which produces an energy spike as the sugar is used, but this quickly leads to a nap-inducing low – pretty heinous if you have a double accountancy lecture to sit through.

So along with natural sugars, we pledge to fill the following pages with gut-sympathetic whole grains so you don't even have to think about it. To help you along your way, see pages 8–9 for a list of whole grains, what their uses are and how to prepare them. (These are simply guidelines and we're sure you'll work out the best quantities to satisfy your tummy rumblings.)

The following flours are an excellent replacement for white flour, although they too can be processed, so try to find products that say 'whole' somewhere on the packet.

- Rye flour
- Buckwheat flour
- Spelt flour

Quinoa

Serving per person (raw weight): 70g

Cooking method: simmer in boiling water for 12 minutes then drain

Nutrition: complex carbs, no fat, some protein

Flavour: nutty flavour goes perfectly with crunchy raw veg

Pearl barley

Serving per person: 80g

Cooking method: boil in water or stock for 40–45 minutes, then drain

Nutrition: loads of fibre and complex carbs

Flavour: tender and light nutty notes perfect to bolster soups and stews

Brown rice

(You may have noticed the slightly Americanised measurements in this recipe – trust us, measuring the water to rice ratio is a lot easier with a mug, y'all.)

Serving per person: ½ mug

Cooking method: soak rice for 10 minutes, drain, tip into a saucepan, pour in ¾ mug of water, bring to the boil, cover and turn heat to the lowest setting. Cook over low heat for 30 minutes, leave to stand, then fluff

Nutrition: complex carbs, high fibre, low protein

Flavour: nutty, works as well cold in a salad as it does as a side to a hot dish

Wholemeal pasta

Serving per person: 80g

Cooking method: bring a generous amount of water to the boil then add the pasta. Cook for 12–18 minutes depending on brand, then drain

Nutrition: complex carbs and fibre

Flavour: Wholesome, deep flavour, use in place of white pasta and enjoy the extra richness

Bulgur wheat

Serving per person: 70g

Cooking method: simmer for 15–18 minutes in boiling water or stock, then drain

Nutrition: high in complex carbs, protein and fibre

Flavour: excellent cold as a salad with dressing and raw veg. Also very good in place of rice in risottos and taking on flavour in stews

Porridge oats

Serving per person: 50g

Cooking method: tip oats into a pan, pour in 300ml of nut milk, cow's milk or water and simmer for about 12 minutes until tender and thick

Nutrition: complex carbs, small amounts of protein and fibre

Flavour: comfortingly bland vehicle for nuts, fruits, honey

Truths and myths cleared up

Macronutrients are broken down into carbohydrates, proteins and fats. These are the nutrients that your body needs to function properly, and just understanding a little about how they work will help you to stay leaner and never end up with that hideous bloated feeling from overeating, as you will always be fuelling your body with what it needs. We will not delve into microscopic detail, but instead here are some very basic rules to follow and some myths to dispel:

Fat is bad for you

Wrong. Fat is absolutely vital for your body to function. From helping to absorb vitamins to forming a necessary component of cell construction, we need fat in our bodies, so don't be afraid. There are different types of fat – from essential fats such as omega-3 to fats that directly increase your cholesterol, such as trans fats. There really is a minefield of information out there to immerse yourself in if you are interested, but very basically, natural fat from sources such as avocados, seeds, nuts, oily fish, butter and even cream is fat that your body knows how to handle. High street fast-food joints serve food that has fat processed into a version of food your body has no idea how to handle, so steer clear unless you like heart burn, diabetes and an ever increasing waistline.

Don't eat carbs especially after 6 p.m.

This is such a load of tosh. Carbohydrates are the main fuel for the muscles in our bodies; we need them, especially if we are doing exercise. If you are on one of those no carb diets and you're not sure why you're so lethargic or why after an initial weight loss you've stopped progressing, it's because you've cut out carbs.

We are by no means saying that you can now graze on all the pasta and bread you want: no, unfortunately it's that word 'moderation' again. Eat small amounts of carbs during the day, and then after exercise – proper exercise that is, not 'walking on the treadmill reading *Grazia*' exercise, but 'heart trying to escape from ribcage' exercise – feel free to eat a massive bowl of pasta with low fat protein to refuel those tired muscles. In fact we're not just saying you can, we're saying you should.

So we all know that, as much as you may complain about never having any money and constantly being broke, from time to time you enjoy a meal out. With this in mind, we were going to rip off some of your favourite restaurant meals and pass them off as our own. However, plagiarism just isn't cool, and we realised it's a lot less work to ask them to do it themselves. So watch out for some recipes scattered throughout this book from our favourite foodie brands as well as the Body Coach Joe Wicks.

Cooking notes

We've stated when a recipe is gluten-free, vegetarian and dairy-free, knowing that the version we make has been created using widely available free-from products. Be sure to check the labels on the ingredients you buy, particularly condiments such as soy sauce, stock cubes and spices (especially curry powder).

Oats are an ingredient to really look at closely as they are often processed in factories that also process wheat and barley, which leads to cross contamination of gluten. Certain brands state that they are totally gluten-free so if you have a serious intolerance then hunt these down.

If you are a vegan and therefore do not eat honey then just swap it with either agave syrup or the slightly more expensive maple syrup.

All eggs are medium-sized and should be cooked from room temperature.

Look out for these symbols:

 Vegetarian   Gluten-free   Dairy-free

Breakfast

It really is time to distance yourself from the Western world's weird fascination with sugar-laden cereals as the breakfast standard. There is barely an honest boxed breakfast out there. Even those marketed as healthy are almost always hiding a sweet secret. Get yourself off the cereals and on to any of the following, which will keep you going through the early morning lectures.

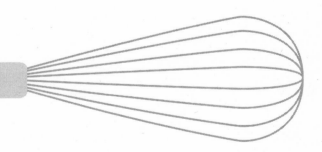

Granola

Makes
about 400g

Cooking time:
30 minutes

Well, we couldn't have written a healthy recipe book without a granola recipe, could we?! There are thousands of granola recipes out there and they are all pretty similar. Our granola stands out because we've sweetened it with apple juice. No need to follow this recipe to the letter: change the dried fruits and seeds to your taste, just keep the quantities of oats and apple juice the same, make sure all the nuts are toasted and all the fruit is added later. Go forth and make granola.

175g gluten-free **rolled oats**
75ml **apple juice**
75g **pumpkin seeds**
50g **sunflower seeds**
25g **sesame seeds**

75g **almonds**
75g **hazelnuts**
100g **dried apricots**, roughly chopped
125g **raisins**

1   Preheat your oven to 180°C (gas mark 4).

2   In a bowl, mix together all the ingredients apart from the apricots and raisins. Tip the mixture on to a large, flat baking tray and spread everything out evenly.

3   Bake the mixture for about 25 minutes, turning a couple of times whilst cooking. The oats, seeds and nuts should all be crunchy and coloured lightly. Remove the tray from the oven and leave to cool completely.

4   When the roasted ingredients are fully cooled to room temperature, tip them into a bowl and mix through the chopped apricots and raisins.

5   The granola will last for about a month in an airtight container, although we think you will eat it much quicker than that.

Lassi porridge

Serves **2**

Cooking time:
25 minutes

Fear not, studentkind, for we are not blending your favourite nineties canine then cooking her up with porridge oats. No, we are combining the best of Scottish breakfasts with the most refreshing of Indian drinks. We always find the best places to pick up the cheapest and tastiest mangoes are the ethnic grocery stores that almost every major city will have. If mango is beyond your budget then just double up the bananas.

300ml **coconut milk**

300ml **water**

5 **cardamom pods**, lightly crushed

100g gluten-free **rolled oats**

2 tsp **vanilla extract**

1 ripe **mango**, peeled and sliced, to serve

1 **banana**, peeled and sliced, to serve

2 tbsp **sunflower seeds**, to serve

2 tbsp **honey**, to serve

1   Pour the coconut milk and water into a saucepan and add the bashed cardamom pods, bring the liquid to the boil and then reduce to a simmer. Tip in the porridge oats and cook for about 10 minutes, stirring regularly until the oats are cooked through and your porridge is nice and thick.

2   Take the porridge off the heat and stir through the vanilla extract.

3   Divvy up the porridge between two bowls and top with the fruit, sunflower seeds and a drizzle of honey.

Smoothie bowl

Serves **4**

Cooking time:
10 minutes

Smoothie bowls are pretty much all the rage at the moment. They basically involve you making a smoothie, tipping it into a bowl and topping it with goodies – a bit like a breakfast soup. It's a great thing to pull out in high summer when fruit is at its best. For variations, think outside the fruit bowl and chuck in some cooked beetroot or avocado.

200g gluten-free **rolled oats**

225g **blueberries**, plus a few extra to go on top

1 **banana**, peeled and roughly chopped

250ml **almond milk**

40g **honey**

Fresh **almonds** roughly chopped, to serve

A few **strawberries**, hulled and sliced, to serve

1   Tip the oats into a bowl and cover with boiling water. Leave them to sit for 5 minutes before draining and leaving to cool.

2   When the oats are cooled to room temperature, put them in a blender with the blueberries, banana, almond milk and honey. Blitz the whole lot together until perfectly smooth and thick.

3   Pour the smoothie into a bowl and top with almonds, strawberries and finally a few blueberries.

4   Get stuck in and feel the warm glow of summer radiate from inside out.

Quinoa power porridge

Serves **4**

Cooking time:
25 minutes

Now here's a breakfast that will keep you fuelled until lunchtime and maybe even through to siesta. The combination of quinoa and classic oats gives your body a super hit of slow release carbs, fibre and a good dose of protein. Chuck a banana on top and you won't need to eat until next week. DO NOT think that quick cook porridge oats are the same as normal porridge oats; they are not. They are processed to within an inch of zero nutritional value – steer clear.

100g **quinoa**

150g gluten-free **rolled oats**

1 **apple**, cored and grated, skin and all

2 tsp **ground cinnamon**

65g **raisins**

1l **almond milk**

2 tbsp **honey**

2 tbsp **pumpkin or sunflower seeds**

Berries, to serve

1 Bring a saucepan of water to the boil, add the quinoa and cook for 7 minutes. Drain the grains immediately.

2 Wipe the saucepan out and chuck the semi-cooked quinoa back in along with all of the other ingredients apart from the honey, the seeds and berries.

3 Bring the almond milk to the boil then reduce the heat to a simmer. Cook the porridge for about 12 minutes, or until the oats are lovely and creamy.

4 Remove the pan from the heat, dole out the porridge into two bowls, pour over the honey, top with the seeds and berries, dig in a spoon and say adios to hunger.

Chia seed brekkie

Serves **2**

Cooking time:
10 minutes,
plus
soaking time

If there was an annual awards ceremony for ingredients, there is no doubt that the best newcomer and general gift to mankind award would have gone to the humble chia seed. Small in size, but packed full of every health benefit out there from omega-3 to fibre, the tiny chia seed punches way above its weight. With health and fashion comes cost and chia seeds can be very expensive, but we promise if you do even a brief amount of research on the internet you will find them sold in bulk and for a reasonable price.

50g **chia seeds**

225ml **almond milk**

1 tbsp **honey**

Blueberries, **blackberries** or **raspberries**, to serve

Nuts and **seeds**, to serve

1   Place the chia seeds in an airtight container like Tupperware or a clean jar. Pour the almond milk over the top and leave to sit for a minimum of 2 hours or up to overnight.

2   When you're ready to eat, just top with honey and your choice of fruit, nuts and seeds.

3   Dig in and feel yourself becoming leaner and healthier with every mouthful.

Overnight oats

Serves **2**

Cooking time:
5 minutes,
plus soaking
overnight

Overnight oats are just a great breakfast, not only because they taste delicious, but also because they satisfy both your mind and body until lunchtime. If you follow the ratios of milk to porridge, you can make almost any combination of flavours your mind can come up with. We think a combination of fruit and nuts makes for the tastiest oats.

125ml **almond milk**

90g **Greek yoghurt**

1 tsp **ground cinnamon**

1 **apple**, cored and grated, skin and all (about 75g)

90g gluten-free **rolled oats**

Drizzle of **honey**

Raisins, to serve

Walnuts, roughly chopped, to serve

1 Whisk together the almond milk, Greek yoghurt and ground cinnamon in a bowl until fully combined.

2 Fold through the apple and the rolled oats. Pour the mixture into an airtight container, like Tupperware or a clean jar. Leave the oats for a minimum of 6 hours, but preferably overnight.

3 When you're ready to eat, drizzle on the honey and scatter over the raisins and walnuts.

Body Coach buckwheat protein pancakes

Serves **1**

Cooking time: **14 minutes**

These cheeky little pancakes taste amazing. Don't be put off by the addition of protein powder – it's a great way of making sure your body is getting the good quality protein it needs to build lean muscle, just ensure the kind you buy is gluten-free.

150g **buckwheat flour**

1 scoop **vanilla protein powder** (about 30g)

1 tsp **baking powder**

200–225ml **almond milk**

1 **egg**

Knob **butter**, for frying

Full fat Greek yoghurt, to serve

1 small handful **blueberries**

Squeeze of **honey**

---

1   Tip the buckwheat flour into a bowl and sprinkle in the protein powder and baking powder.

2   Beat together the almond milk with the egg until totally combined and then gradually pour the liquid into the dry ingredients, stirring as you go to avoid lumps. Beat everything together until you have a batter the consistency of very thick double cream.

3   Heat the butter in a non-stick frying pan over a medium to high heat. When melted and bubbling, spoon large blobs of the mixture (roughly a heaped tablespoon) into the pan and using the back of the spoon, flatten them to form a circle.

4   Don't overcrowd the pan – I normally fry 3–4 at a time.

...

5 Fry the pancakes for about 2 minutes on one side or until you see bubbles coming to the surface of the batter and then popping, flip and then cook for a further 2 minutes on the other side. Remove the cooked pancakes on to a piece of kitchen roll to get rid of any excess oil.

6 Repeat the process with the remaining batter until you have a small pile of pancakes in front of you.

7 Stack the pancakes high, blob on the yoghurt, scatter over the blueberries and drizzle over a little honey.

Baked eggs

Serves **2**

Cooking time:
20 minutes

Eggs are without doubt the most popular breakfast alternative to sugary cereals, which makes sense as we really can't think of any negatives to the humble oeuf. They are perfectly packaged in their own shell, have a long shelf life without refrigeration, can be prepared a million and one ways, are filled with protein and good fats, and are cheap. Go out and spread the eggy love.

---

2 large handfuls **baby spinach**
½ 400g tin of **chopped tomatoes**
1½ tsp **smoked paprika**

½ tsp **ground cumin**
3 tbsp **kidney beans**
4 **eggs**

---

1   Preheat your oven to 190°C (gas mark 5).

2   Put a kettle on to boil and empty the spinach into a colander. Pour the boiling water over the spinach to wilt. Run cold water over the leaves to cool them and then pick them up and squeeze out the excess liquid.

3   Ping the tomatoes in the microwave for 1 minute, just to take the cold edge off them and then stir through the wilted spinach, paprika, cumin and kidney beans. Spoon the mixture either into 4 small ramekins (mugs will work as well) or into one large, shallow ovenproof dish.

4   Make a small gap in the tomato mixture, crack an egg in each, place the ramekins/mugs/dish on to a tray and slide into the oven. Bake the eggs for 12–15 minutes, or until the yolk and white are cooked as you like.

Scrambled tofu

Serves **2**

Cooking time:
20 minutes

Believe us when we say we were a little sceptical of this combination of words too. Sure enough there are some terrible versions of scrambled tofu out there, but this one is really tasty, we promise. Our secret is that if we want scrambled eggs we'll use eggs. This isn't trying to be a substitute; it's a recipe in its own right.

½ tbsp **coconut** or **vegetable oil**

½ **red pepper**, de-seeded and cut into ½ cm strips

40g **kale** leaves, tough stalks removed

1 **tomato**, roughly chopped

2 tsp **garam masala**

1 tsp **smoked paprika**

400g **firm tofu**

Wholemeal toast, to serve

1   Heat the oil in a frying pan over a medium heat. When hot, add the red pepper and the kale. Fry the vegetables, stirring regularly for about 10 minutes by which time they should have softened nicely. Scrape in the tomato and sprinkle in the garam masala and smoked paprika.

2   Fry the ingredients, stirring almost constantly for 1 minute, and then add a splash of water and continue to cook for a further 5 minutes, or until the tomato chunks begin to break down a little.

3   Roughly chop the tofu and add to the pan. Use a wooden spoon to break the tofu into small pieces (to resemble scrambled egg) as you stir. Cook the whole lot together for 2–3 minutes, or until you are happy the tofu is warmed through.

4   Dish up on toast to a mate and wait for their reaction.

Spiced beans on toast

Serves **2**

Cooking time:
15 minutes

Those famous baked beans out there are admittedly delicious, but also full of sugar and preservatives. So here is our version, a bit smokier, but a lot delicious. To make this gluten-free, simply swap the wholemeal for gluten-free toast.

½ tbsp **coconut** or **vegetable oil**

1 **shallot** or ½ **onion**, peeled and diced

2 tsp **smoked paprika**

1 tbsp **tomato purée**

2 tsp **vinegar** (red wine or balsamic)

1 x 410g tin **cannellini beans**, drained and rinsed

100ml **water**

2 slices **wholemeal toast**, to serve

1 Heat the oil in a saucepan over a medium to high heat. When hot, add the diced shallot and fry for 2 minutes. Sprinkle in the smoked paprika and fry, stirring almost constantly for 1 minute with the onions.

2 Squeeze in the tomato purée and mix with the other ingredients. Pour in the vinegar and let it bubble away to almost nothing. Tip in the cannellini beans along with about 100ml of water. Bring the whole lot to the boil and simmer for 8 minutes by which time the beans should be lovely and soft and the sauce thickened.

3 Pile up the beans on toasted wholemeal bread.

Body Coach bacon and mushroom omelette

Serves **1**

Cooking time: **12 minutes**

When you're not exercising, fat is a great fuel for your body. Almost any non-processed fat can be used as fuel, from butter to double cream – they really can form part of a healthy lifestyle. This omelette just goes to show that making healthy choices doesn't mean you miss out on tasty food.

Knob **butter**

2 rashers **back bacon**, cut into 1cm strips

5 **mushrooms**, roughly chopped into quarters

1 **red chilli**, de-seeded and finely sliced

1 large handful **baby spinach**

3 **eggs**

30g **cheddar**, grated

Small **salad**, to serve

Pepper

1 Heat the butter in a medium non-stick frying pan over a medium to high heat. When melted and bubbling, chuck in the bacon and mushrooms and fry, stirring regularly for about 3 minutes, or until you are happy the bacon is fully cooked through.

2 Toss in the chilli and fry along with the bacon and mushrooms for another minute before throwing in the baby spinach and wilting it right down.

3 Beat together the eggs with a small pinch of pepper and then pour into the frying pan.

4 Carefully stir everything together and then make your omelette by drawing in the cooked edges with a wooden spoon or spatula, letting the raw egg run into the space you've created at the side of the pan. Continue the process until the majority of the egg is cooked through.

5 Sprinkle the cheese over half of the omelette and fry for 30 seconds more before folding it in half and tipping out on to a plate. Serve up your omelette with a nice side salad.

Smoked haddock and spinach omelette

Serves **1**

Cooking time:
15 minutes

In our opinion, eggs really are the original superfood. They are filled with protein and those all important fats that power little grey cells. Combine with the cheap and protein-packed smoked haddock and what we have here is a little slice of breakfast heaven.

---

1 tbsp **coconut** or **vegetable oil**

150g **smoked haddock**, skin removed and flesh cut into 1cm cubes

2 **spring onions**, topped, tailed and finely sliced

1 large handful **baby spinach**

3 **eggs**

Salt and pepper

---

1   Heat the oil in a small non-stick frying pan over a medium to high heat. When hot, add the smoked haddock and stir-fry for 1 minute by which time the fish will be virtually cooked through. Add the spring onions and toss together with the fish, continue to cook for one more minute.

2   Throw in the baby spinach and toss it in the pan until it has totally wilted. Beat the eggs adding a pinch of both salt and pepper and pour them into the pan.

3   Make your omelette by drawing in the cooked edges with a wooden spoon or spatula, letting the raw egg run into the space you've created at the side of the pan. Continue the process until the majority of the egg is cooked through.

4   Stop stirring and allow the egg to set and colour on the base of the pan for about 45 seconds. Expertly fold the omelette in half, slide on to a plate and enjoy one of the simplest, tastiest combinations in the culinary world.

Prawn omelette

Serves **1**

Cooking time:
10 minutes

The omelette: tried, tested and always delicious. Here is a variation you may not have tried yet, using soy and sesame to flavour the eggs. I've suggested prawns as the protein here, but they can be expensive, so if you're on a budget try using cooked turkey instead.

3 **eggs**

3 tsp **light soy sauce** or **tamari**

2 tsp toasted **sesame oil**

½ tbsp **coconut** or **vegetable oil**

125g cooked **prawns**

1 large handful **baby spinach**

1 **red chilli**, de-seeded and finely sliced, to serve

25g **cashew nuts**, roughly chopped, to serve

1   Crack the eggs into a bowl and pour in the soy sauce or tamari and the sesame oil. Whisk the ingredients together until they are well mixed.

2   Heat the oil in a small non-stick frying pan over a high heat. When melted and hot add the prawns and stir-fry for 30 seconds, until you are happy they are warmed through. Chuck in the baby spinach and toss with the prawns until the leaves are wilted.

3   Pour the egg mixture into the pan. Make your omelette by drawing in the cooked edges with a wooden spoon or spatula, letting the raw egg run into the space you've created at the side of the pan. Continue the process until the majority of the egg is cooked through. Stop stirring and allow the egg to set and colour on the base of the pan for about 45 seconds.

4   Remove the pan from the heat, slide the omelette on to a plate and top with the chilli and the cashew nuts.

Chorizo, tomatoes, kale and eggs

Serves **1**

Cooking time:
15 minutes

Not such a catchy title, but a dish that we reckon you will be cooking variations of at least once a week. If you are a vegetarian but don't want to lose the flavour of chorizo then just add 2 tsp smoked paprika. We've called this recipe gluten-free as the chorizo we buy from our supermarket doesn't contain gluten, but if you have an intolerance, be sure to check the packaging.

½ tbsp **coconut** or **sunflower oil**

75g **chorizo**, roughly chopped into 1cm pieces

2 **spring onions**, topped, tailed and sliced thinly

½ **red pepper**, de-seeded and sliced thinly

75g **kale**, woody stalks removed

5 **cherry tomatoes**, sliced in half

2 **eggs**

1 tbsp chopped **parsley** (optional), to serve

1 Heat the oil in a small frying pan over a medium to high heat. When hot and melted, add the chorizo, spring onions, red pepper, kale and cherry tomatoes. Fry the ingredients, tossing them regularly for 5 minutes, or until they begin to soften.

2 Reduce the heat to medium and fashion two small gaps in the cooking ingredients with a wooden spoon. Crack the eggs into the gaps and then put a lid on the pan (if you don't have a lid that will fit then just slide a plate over the top). Let the ingredients cook under the lid for 2 minutes.

3 Remove the lid, sprinkle over the parsley and eat straight from the frying pan . . . or decant on to a plate if you have any self control!

Chorizo, sweetcorn and sweet potato hash

Serves **1**

Cooking time: **15 minutes**

A tin of sweetcorn and a microwave – you can't get much more student-friendly than that surely. Where others smirk at the humble microwave, we've always seen it as a miracle device: it cooks things quickly, without mess and doesn't leach out nutrients whilst zapping them. We've called this recipe gluten-free as the chorizo and chilli sauce we buy from the supermarket doesn't contain gluten, but if you have an intolerance, be sure to check the packaging.

---

1 **sweet potato**, scrubbed clean

1 tbsp **coconut** or **vegetable oil**

50g **chorizo**, roughly chopped into 2cm pieces

2 **spring onions**, topped, tailed and finely sliced

100g tinned **sweetcorn**, drained

1 large handful **baby spinach**

1 **egg**

½ bunch **coriander**, to serve (optional)

Chilli sauce, to serve (optional)

Salt and pepper

---

1   Roughly chop the sweet potato in to 3cm chunks, place them in a microwave-proof dish and then zap in the microwave at full power (900w) for 3 minutes, leave to rest for 1 minute and then zap for a further 3 minutes and again leave to rest for 1 minute. The sweet potato should be tender, but still holding their shape by now, if not then just zap for another couple of minutes.

2   Heat half of the oil in a small frying pan over a medium to high heat. When hot add the chorizo and spring onion and fry for 2 minutes. Crank up the heat to maximum and when everything is sizzling, add the cooked sweet potato. Fry all the ingredients together for about 3 minutes, or until the sweet potato has taken on a little colour.

•••

3 Finally reduce the heat to medium again and tumble in the sweetcorn and baby spinach leaves. Toss everything together, seasoning with salt and pepper, until the kernels are warmed through and the spinach is wilted.

4 Spoon the hash on to a plate, wipe the pan out with a piece of kitchen roll and then heat the remaining oil over a high heat. When hot, carefully crack in the egg and fry to your liking. Quickly whip the egg out and sit it proudly atop your hash.

5 Sprinkle with coriander and a squirt of your favourite hot sauce before saying 'thank you' to your microwave and devouring.

Lunch

These are the lighter dishes that we think are not only pretty simple to cook up, but also easy to pack up, transport and eat at room temperature, meaning you won't have to rely on the overpriced fare from the campus canteens. Many of these dishes can be easily doubled up to feed more hungry minds.

Ginger and edamame rice bowl

Serves **2**

Cooking time:
1 hour

Ah, the glorious rice bowl. Before the healthy-eating trend came about, millions of people had just been calling it a bowl of rice, but now we must call it a rice bowl and treat it as if it were recently invented. To be honest, this is just a bowl of tasty stuff that will make you live longer and appear more attractive to the opposite sex. True dat.

1 mug **brown basmati** rice

1½ mugs **water**, plus extra for soaking

150g frozen **edamame beans**

4 **baby sweetcorn**, sliced in half lengthways

3cm fresh **ginger**

2 tsp **sesame oil**

1½ tbsp **vinegar** (rice, white wine or cider)

2 tbsp **light soy sauce** or **tamari**

4 **radishes**, roughly chopped into quarters

2 handfuls **watercress**

1 Tip the brown rice into a bowl and cover with some water. Leave the rice to sit for 10 minutes before draining through a sieve, tipping into a small saucepan and covering with 1½ mugs of water.

2 Place the pan over a high heat and bring the water to the boil, immediately cover the pan with a lid and reduce the heat to its very lowest setting. Leave the rice to cook like this for 30 minutes, turn off the heat and leave to sit for a further 5 minutes.

3 Whilst the rice is cooking, heat another pan of water and when boiling, drop in the edamame beans and sweetcorn and simmer for 3–4 minutes or until the sweetcorn is just tender and the edamame are heated through. Drain the vegetables through a sieve, and cool under cold water.

...

4 Take the piece of ginger and grate it straight on to a clean J-cloth or similar material. When you have grated it, gather up the cloth around the ginger and squeeze the juice from the nugget straight into a bowl. Pour in the sesame oil, vinegar and soy sauce or tamari, and mix well.

5 When you are happy the rice is cooked, remove the lid and fluff with a fork. Pour half of the dressing into the hot rice and stir through, then divide the rice between two bowls.

6 Top the rice with the edamame, baby sweetcorn, radishes and watercress and then drizzle the remaining dressing. Yum.

7 You could totally invent a new fad by serving this on a plate.

Mushroom and spinach pasta

Serves **2**

Cooking time:
20 minutes

Ah, such a classic from the old days of home economics classes when the bearded lady at the front of the room would demonstrate how to peel a mushroom with her wart-ridden fingers and then try to convince you to taste the food from the same cutlery she had just used. Urgh, we think we might have spoiled the recipe with that image in our minds. Go swill your brains out and come back to make this winner of a dish.

160g dried **wholemeal spaghetti**
1 tbsp **coconut** or **vegetable oil**
½ **onion**, peeled and diced
300g **mushrooms** (we like chestnut)
2 cloves **garlic**, peeled and diced

2 sprigs **thyme**
1 **lemon**
2 large handfuls **baby spinach**
Salt and pepper

1   Put a large pan of water on to heat and when boiling, slide in your wholemeal spaghetti. Cook the pasta according to the packet instructions.

2   Whilst the pasta is cooking, heat the oil in a medium saucepan over a medium to high heat. When hot, chuck in the onion and fry for about 3 minutes, stirring every now and then. Roughly chop the mushrooms into sixths and crank the heat right up under the saucepan.

3   Add the mushrooms and fry with the onion for about a minute or until the mushrooms have taken on a little colour. Add the diced garlic and the fresh thyme sprigs and continue to stir and fry for one more minute.

...

4 Now reduce the heat to medium and place a lid on top of the saucepan. Stew the mushrooms like this for 5 minutes, by which time the ingredients should all be cooked through and the mushrooms will have leaked out and then reabsorbed their delicious cooking liquids.

5 Take the lid off and increase the heat to maximum again to evaporate any excess liquid there might be around. Squeeze in the juice from the lemon and follow quickly with the baby spinach leaves. Cook the ingredients until the spinach has completely wilted.

6 Drain the pasta through a colander and add to the mushroom pan. Toss the whole lot together along with a decent pinch of salt and pepper.

7 Serve up and scoff down.

Bill's Israeli couscous salad

Serves **4–6**

Preparation time: **10 minutes**

Cooking time: **30 minutes**

This colourful and wholesome salad combines griddled asparagus with fresh spinach, olives, kidney beans and Israeli couscous, which has a nutty flavour and smooth texture and can be used in place of normal couscous, pasta or rice in any dish. Serve alongside other salads to create a mezze spread if enjoying with friends or split into portions for an easy and delicious mid-week lunch. It will keep in the fridge for a few days.

1 tsp **turmeric**

250g **Israeli couscous**

50ml **white wine vinegar**

Juice 2 **lemons**

125g **asparagus**

3 tbsp **olive oil**

2 tbsp **pesto** (see page 44)

1 x 410g tin of **kidney beans**, drained and rinsed

200g fresh **spinach** leaves

275g large **olives**, stoned

1 handful **parsley**, to serve (optional)

Mixed seeds, to serve (optional)

Salt and pepper

1   Bring a large pan of water to the boil. Add the turmeric and couscous, then simmer for 20 minutes. Drain well and, whilst still hot, stir in the vinegar and lemon juice. Cover and leave to cool.

2   Whilst you're getting the griddle pan good and hot, trim any tough ends from the asparagus, then coat the spears in 1 tbsp of the olive oil. Griddle for 5–10 minutes until crispy.

3   Stir the pesto and remaining olive oil together in a jug, season with salt and freshly ground black pepper and pour this dressing over the couscous. Mix in the kidney beans, spinach and olives. To serve, place the mixture in a wide, shallow dish and top with the griddled asparagus.

4   You can sprinkle some roughly chopped parsley across the top and/or a couple of tablespoons of crunchy seeds.

Pasta with rocket pesto

Serves **1**

Cooking time:
20 minutes

This is the sort of recipe to pull out of the cupboard when you're waiting for your pay cheque to come through. It's cheap, super-tasty and does not skimp on flavour. We've left out Parmesan from this recipe, but if you do like a bit of cheese in your pesto and can't afford the classic Parmesan, then try using a mature cheddar.

80g dried **wholemeal spaghetti**

30g **rocket**

1 small bunch **basil**, roughly chopped

½ clove **garlic**, peeled and
  roughly chopped

75ml **olive oil**

Juice ½ **lemon**

Salt and pepper

1 Bring a pan of water to the boil. Drop in your spaghetti and cook to packet instructions. Just before draining, remove about a quarter of a mug of cooking liquid and keep to one side.

2 Whilst the pasta is cooking, place the rocket, basil, garlic, olive oil and lemon juice into a food processor along with a good pinch of both salt and pepper. Give the ingredients a little blitz.

3 When the pasta is cooked and you have saved a little of the cooking liquid, strain the pasta through a colander and leave to drain. Pour the saved hot pasta water into the processor with the rocket and other ingredients and blitz the whole lot together until smooth.

4 Tip the pasta into the cooking pan, scrape in the pesto and toss the whole lot together.

5 Plate up and feel the warmth of comfort with every mouthful.

Superpower salad

Serves **2**

Cooking time:
40 minutes

This recipe should come with a cape, it's so potent. This is to be made on days when the sun is shining and you want to reward your bodies for their years of phlegmatic and total loyalty to every whim of your crazy brain.

---

1 raw **beetroot**, scrubbed and roughly cut into 8 wedges

1 **sweet potato**, scrubbed and roughly cut into 8 wedges

1 **red onion**, peeled and roughly cut into 8 wedges

4 tbsp **olive oil**

20g **almonds**

15g **pine nuts**

Juice 1 **lemon**

1 large handful **baby spinach**

1 handful **watercress**

15g **pumpkin seeds**

100g **pomegranate seeds**

Salt and pepper

---

1 Preheat your oven to 200°C (gas mark 6).

2 Put the beetroot, sweet potato and red onion into a bowl and pour over 2 tbsp of the olive oil and a generous pinch of both salt and pepper. Toss the whole lot together until you are happy the ingredients are well slicked.

3 Tip the veg on to a roasting tray, slip into the oven and roast for 30 minutes, turning halfway through the cooking process. After 25 minutes, add the almonds and pine nuts and roast along with the veg.

4 After 30 minutes, the veg should be lightly coloured and tender. If so, remove from the oven, scrape into a bowl and leave to cool a little.

•••

5 Whisk together the lemon juice with the remaining olive oil until the two are well combined into a dressing. Pour half of the dressing over the cooling veg and toss to coat.

6 Pile the dressed veg up on a plate, top with the spinach, watercress, pumpkin seeds and pomegranate seeds. Finish with a pinch of salt and pepper and the last of the dressing.

Pea and butter bean soup

Serves **4–6**

Cooking time:
30 minutes

This soup could well be the source of the Incredible Hulk's strength and colour. Brimming with minerals and antioxidants from the fresh veg and herbs, this is one for when you feel you are coming down with something and need to stop the excess.

---

2 tbsp **coconut** or **vegetable oil**

1 **leek**, topped, tailed and cut into 1cm rings

1 small **onion**, peeled and diced

3 × 400g cans of **butter beans**, drained and rinsed

1l **vegetable stock**

250g frozen **peas**

1 small bunch **parsley**, leaves only

1 small bunch **mint**, leaves only

1 handful **spinach**

Juice ½ **lemon**

Salt and pepper

---

1 Heat the oil in a large saucepan over a medium to high heat. When hot, add the leek and onion and fry for 6–7 minutes, stirring regularly, until the onion and leek have softened.

2 Tip in the butter beans and stir with the rest of the ingredients. Pour in the stock and bring to the boil. Simmer the liquid for 12 minutes by which time the butter beans should be almost falling to pieces.

3 Add the frozen peas, parsley, mint and spinach, bring the whole lot back to the boil and simmer for 1 minute. Blitz the ingredients with a stick or jug blender until smooth and finish with a squeeze of fresh lemon juice and a good pinch of salt and pepper.

Miso-glazed aubergine and quinoa

Serves **2**

Cooking time:
40 minutes

Aubergines very often seem to be the go-to vegetable for vegetarians, and we can quite see why. A little like mushrooms they have a wonderful capacity to absorb flavour and also to retain a satisfying texture once cooked. We've teamed them up with a classic miso glaze which adds wonderful umami to the tender flesh.

---

2 medium **aubergines**

3 tbsp **vegetable oil**

1½ tbsp **miso paste**

1 tbsp **honey**

2 cloves **garlic**, peeled and finely chopped

3 tsp **sesame oil**

50ml **water**

200g **quinoa**

¼ **cucumber**, de-seeded, topped, tailed and cut in half lengthways

1 tbsp **vinegar** (rice or white wine)

3 **spring onions**, topped, tailed and finely sliced

6 **radishes**, topped, tailed and roughly cut into quarters

1 tbsp **olive oil**

40g **roasted peanuts**, roughly chopped, to serve

Salt and pepper

---

1 Preheat your oven to 190°C (gas mark 5).

2 Take each aubergine in turn and slice in half lengthways. Carefully score the flesh of the aubergine all over, cutting deep, but ensuring you don't pierce the skin. Lay a piece of baking parchment or foil on a baking tray and place the aubergine halves on top, flesh side up. Drizzle with the vegetable oil and then bake in the oven for 25 minutes to give them a head start.

3 Whilst the aubergines are cooking, splat the miso into a bowl and follow it with the honey, garlic, sesame oil and about 50ml of water. Give the whole lot a good mix until you reach a smooth paste.

•••

4 When the aubergines have had their 25 minutes, remove them from the oven and smear the miso glaze over liberally. Slide the aubergines back into the oven, reduce the temperature to 170°C (gas mark 3) and cook for a further 20 minutes, or until the aubergines are tender.

5 Whilst the aubergines are cooking, put the quinoa in boiling water and cook according to the packet instructions. When cooked, drain through a sieve and cool under cold running water. Drain again and then tip the cooled grains into a large bowl. Slice the cucumber halves into half-moon shapes and chuck into the quinoa along with the vinegar, spring onions, radishes, olive oil and a good pinch of both salt and pepper. Mix the whole lot until it is all well combined.

6 Remove the cooked aubergines from the oven. Pile the quinoa salad up on two plates, top with the aubergine halves and finally sprinkle with the peanuts.

Cauliflower and sweet potato soup

Serves **4**

Cooking time:
40 minutes

Both of these vegetables have such a wholesome and velvet-like texture when cooked and puréed into a soup. They also both have a great affinity with curry flavour, so this just seems a very natural recipe to put together.

1 tbsp **coconut** or **vegetable oil**

1 large **onion**, peeled and roughly diced into small pieces

3cm **ginger**, peeled and roughly chopped

1½ tbsp **mild curry powder**

1 small **cauliflower**, florets only, roughly chopped

2 **sweet potatoes**, peeled and roughly chopped into 2cm chunks

400ml **coconut milk**

600ml **vegetable stock** (you may need a little more depending on veg size)

Small bunch **coriander**, roughly chopped, to serve

Salt and pepper

1 Heat the oil in a large saucepan over a medium to high heat. When hot, tip in the onion and ginger. Fry the ingredients, stirring regularly for 5 minutes, or until the onion has softened. Sprinkle in the curry powder and fry along with the ginger and onion for 1 minute.

2 Chuck in the cauliflower florets and the sweet potato chunks. Stir in to mix with all the other cooking ingredients.

3 Pour in the coconut milk and the vegetable stock. The liquid should just about cover the vegetables. Season with a little salt and pepper, bring the whole lot up to the boil and then simmer for 25–30 minutes, by which time the vegetables should all be incredibly soft.

4 Blitz up the soup with a stick or in a jug blender, taste and adjust the seasoning.

5 Serve up your soup with freshly chopped coriander.

Ma Po tofu

Serves **2**

Cooking time:
25 minutes

Tofu often receives a bad rep and we're not totally sure why. Perhaps people think it's bland, perhaps people think it's slimy – who knows. What we know is that it is an incredible source of meat-free protein that contains virtually no fat. For all of you who think tofu dishes are tasteless, this dish will blow the socks off your preconceptions. Serve on plain rice for an incredibly filling meal. To make this recipe gluten-free, ensure you use gluten-free black bean sauce and tamari.

---

1 tbsp **coconut** or **vegetable oil**

4 **spring onions**, topped and tailed

6 **shiitake mushrooms**, roughly chopped into small pieces

2 cloves **garlic**, peeled and finely chopped

1 **red chilli**, de-seeded and finely sliced

1 **green pepper**, de-seeded and cut into 2cm squares

2 tbsp **black bean sauce**

100ml **vegetable stock**

1½ tbsp **light soy sauce** or **tamari**

400g **silken tofu**, roughly chopped or spooned into bite-sized pieces

2 tsp **sesame oil**

Brown rice, to serve

---

1 Heat the oil in a large frying pan over a medium to high heat. Take the spring onions and cut the green part from the white. Save the green and finely slice up the white, adding it to the oil as soon as it is hot.

2 Chuck in the shiitake mushrooms, garlic, red chilli and green pepper and stir-fry the whole lot together for about 2 minutes, or until the mushrooms just start to soften.

3 Dollop in the black bean sauce quickly followed by the vegetable stock. Bring the whole lot up to the boil and simmer for 2 minutes.

...

4 Pour in the soy sauce or tamari and carefully add the tofu. Simmer for about 1 minute or until you are happy the tofu is warmed all the way through.

5 Finely slice the green part of the spring onion saved from earlier and scatter over the bubbling tofu. Take the pan from the heat, drizzle over the sesame oil and serve atop steaming piles of brown rice.

Sweet potato stir-fry

Serves **2**

Cooking time:
15 minutes

The name 'sweet potato' makes it sound like the devil's own food. Sugary sweetness delivered on the back of starchy potato – really? Well, actually even though the orange flesh is high in natural sugars and starch, most of it is delivered in the form of dietary fibre which actually helps our bodies regulate sugar levels. Add to that high levels of vitamins C and A and suddenly the sweet potato becomes our best friend.

½ tbsp **coconut** or **vegetable oil**

1 tsp **cumin seeds**

1 tsp **mustard seeds** (brown or black)

1 **red onion**, peeled and finely diced

1 **sweet potato** (about 400g), peeled and cut into 1cm cubes

2 cloves **garlic**, peeled and finely diced

3cm **ginger**, peeled and finely diced

1 **red chilli**, de-seeded and finely sliced

2 tsp **smoked paprika**

1 tsp **ground turmeric**

50ml **water**

2 medium **tomatoes**, roughly chopped into 2cm chunks

2 large handfuls **baby spinach**

Juice 1 **lime**

Salt and pepper

---

1   Heat the oil in a large frying pan over a medium to high heat. When hot, spoon in the cumin and mustard seeds, fry for 30 seconds and then scrape in the red onion and sweet potato. Fry the ingredients all together, stirring regularly for about 4 minutes, or until the onion just starts to soften and the potato takes on a little colour.

2   Add the garlic, ginger and red chilli and continue stir-frying for 2 minutes. Sprinkle in the paprika and turmeric and fry, stirring almost constantly for 20 seconds.

•••

3 Pour in about 50ml of water and add the tomato chunks and a generous pinch of salt and pepper. Mix the whole lot together and cook out for about 8 minutes, or until the tomatoes are collapsed and the sweet potato is tender. Keep an eye on the pan adding water every now and then to stop the pan from 'cooking dry'.

4 When you are happy that the potato is tender, stir through the baby spinach allowing it to wilt in the heat of the stew.

5 Remove your pan from the heat and squeeze over the lime juice. Serve up your quick and easy curry and watch as your lucky friend falls in love with your cooking.

Barley and root veg broth

Serves **4**

Cooking time:
45 minutes

There's no more satisfying feeling than cooking ingredients that are good for you in a stock that is also good for you. It's like goodness squared. This is one for the deepest darkest months when you're low on energy and want a bowl of broth that is going to reinvigorate you and give you the biggest of gastro hugs.

1 tbsp **coconut** or **vegetable oil**

1 **leek**, topped, tailed, washed and cut into 2cm chunks

1 large **carrot**, topped, tailed, peeled and cut into 1cm chunks

2 **parsnips**, topped, tailed, peeled and cut into 1cm chunks

1 medium **potato**, peeled and cut into 1cm chunks

1 tbsp **tomato purée**

90g **pearl barley**

2 sprigs **thyme**

1.2l **chicken stock**

2 handfuls **kale**, stalks removed

1 small bunch **parsley**, roughly chopped

Juice ½ **lemon**

1   Heat the oil in a large saucepan over a medium to high heat. When hot, add the leek, carrot, parsnips and potato and fry, stirring regularly for 2 minutes, until the leek just starts to soften.

2   Add the tomato purée and stir in to the already cooking ingredients. Continue to stir and fry for 1 minute.

3   Add the pearl barley and thyme sprigs and stir in to the rest of the ingredients. Pour in the chicken stock and bring up to the boil. Simmer the broth, uncovered, for about 40 minutes, by which time the vegetables should all be very soft, and the pearl barley swollen and cooked through.

4   Add the kale and continue to cook for a further 3–4 minutes, just long enough for the kale to cook through.

5   Serve up steaming bowls of restorative broth with a generous topping of parsley and a cheeky squeeze of lemon juice.

Veggie and feta frittata

Serves **2**

Cooking time:
20 minutes

The frittata should become a once-a-week staple in your household. Not only is it nutritious and cheap, but it also tastes great cold the next day and is easily transported and simple to consume without the hassle of knives and forks – all you need is hand and mouth coordination.

1 tbsp **coconut** or **vegetable oil**

1 **sweet potato**, scrubbed and grated

1 **courgette**, washed and grated

2 large handfuls **baby spinach**

6 **eggs**

75g **feta**

50g **walnuts**, roughly broken up

Small **salad**, to serve (optional)

Salt and pepper

1   Heat the oil in a good quality, medium, non-stick frying pan over a medium heat. When hot, add the grated sweet potato and the courgette and cook, stirring regularly for 6–7 minutes, or until the grated strands are soft.

2   Turn your grill on to maximum.

3   Increase the heat on the hob to maximum and add the handfuls of spinach. Mix the leaves in with the other vegetables and cook just long enough for them to wilt.

4   Crack the eggs into a bowl and whisk them together with a pinch of salt and pepper. Pour the beaten eggs into the pan and make your omelette by drawing in the cooked edges with a wooden spoon or spatula, letting the raw egg run into the space you've created at the side of the pan. Continue the process until the majority of the egg is cooked through.

•••

5 Stop stirring and allow the egg to set and colour on the base of the pan for about 45 seconds. Crumble the feta over the top and slide your frying pan under the grill. If your pan has a plastic handle, make sure it doesn't go under the element or you will ruin your pan.

6 Grill the frittata for about 2 minutes, or until the egg on top is completely cooked through and the feta is melting and turning golden brown.

7 Remove the pan from the grill, slide the frittata out and scatter with the walnuts. Serve up with a salad and eat secretly away from your housemates otherwise they'll want some too.

Falafel hash

Serves **2**

Cooking time:
20 minutes

Ah, the wondrous falafel, a thing of mystic beauty. Its roots are firmly in the Middle East, yet its popularity has been spread worldwide by devoted vegetarians. And now it is the turn of university campuses, with this, our new version. When we say new, we really mean lazy; instead of shaping and frying the little beauties we literally just chuck all the ingredients into a pan and fry them up together: so much more simple.

---

1 tbsp **coconut** or **vegetable oil**

1 **red onion**, peeled and diced

2 cloves **garlic**, peeled and diced

1 **red chilli**, de-seeded and finely chopped

2 tsp **ground cumin**

2 tsp **smoked paprika**

1 **tomato**, roughly chopped into 8 chunks

1 **carrot**, peeled and grated

1 × 400g tin of **chickpeas**, drained and rinsed

1 bunch **coriander**, roughly chopped

4 tbsp **Greek yoghurt**

Juice 1 **lemon**

2 **wholemeal pitta breads** or wraps

Salt and pepper

---

1 Heat the oil in a large frying pan over a medium to high heat. When hot, add the diced red onion and fry, stirring regularly for 2 minutes and then chuck in the garlic and red chilli and fry for a further minute.

2 Sprinkle in the ground spices and stir into the onion and garlic. Cook out the spices for 30 seconds and then add the tomato and carrot. Fry the ingredients together, stirring regularly for 2–3 minutes by which time everything should be just cooked through. Tumble in the chickpeas and fry for 2 minutes, or until you are happy that they are fully heated through.

•••

3 Take the pan off the heat and stir through the coriander along with a decent pinch of salt and pepper.

4 Mix the Greek yoghurt and lemon juice together with a pinch of salt and pepper.

5 Toast the pittas and slice open, stuff the pittas full of the falafel mix, then drizzle over the zesty yoghurt.

6 Et voilà, you are now uber trendy.

Broccoli and tofu soup

Serves **4**

Cooking time:
20 minutes

You don't like tofu? We don't care because in this recipe you won't even taste it. We've used silken tofu here to not only thicken the soup, but also to add a good dose of protein to your bowl. Give the recipe a go and it won't be long before you start dropping tofu into more of your soups. True dat.

1 tbsp **coconut** or **vegetable oil**

1 **onion**, peeled and diced

2 heads of **broccoli**, florets removed from stalk

1 **potato**, peeled and diced

4 **eggs**

1¼ l **vegetable stock**

200g **silken tofu**, roughly scooped or chopped

1 large handful **spinach**

3 tsp **sesame oil**

Chilli flakes (optional)

Salt and pepper

1 Heat the oil in a large saucepan over a medium to high heat. When hot, add the onion and begin to sweat. Take the broccoli stalk and chop it into 1cm pieces, putting the florets to one side. Add the stalk to the pan with the sweating onion and chuck the potato in too. Sweat the vegetables, stirring regularly for 5 minutes by which time the onion should have softened.

2 Pour in the stock and bring the whole lot to the boil. Simmer the ingredients for 8–10 minutes, or until the vegetables are very soft.

3 When you are happy that the potatoes, onions and broccoli stalk are fully cooked through, add the florets and continue simmering until they too are tender – about 5 minutes.

•••

4 Whilst the soup is bubbling away, bring a second pot of water to the boil. When boiling, turn the temperature right down and carefully crack the eggs in. Don't let the water boil, just keep it at a very low simmer and cook the eggs for about 4 minutes for soft yolks.

5 Whilst the eggs are cooking, add the tofu and spinach to the soup ingredients, bring to the boil one last time and then blitz with a jug or hand blender until smooth. Season well with salt and pepper and then ladle into bowls.

6 Slide a poached egg into each of the soups and finish with a little drizzle of sesame oil and a pinch of chilli flakes.

Roast veg and lentil salad

Serves **2**

Cooking time:
25 minutes

Roasting vegetables not only concentrates the flavours but also safeguards many of the nutrients whilst giving your mouth a delicious, crunchy texture that is far more satisfying than their boiled counterparts. If you are not a fan of anchovies, or want to keep this a vegetarian gluten-free dish, then just replace the anchovies with 1–2 tbsp tamari. Top the dish with a poached egg to make it more substantial.

150g **puy lentils**

1 head **broccoli**, florets only

1 **courgette**, topped, tailed and cut into 2cm thick half moons

8 **radishes**, sliced in half

2 tbsp **olive oil**

4 jarred **anchovy fillets**, drained and roughly chopped

1 sprig **rosemary**, leaves only

1 **red chilli**, de-seeded and sliced

1½ tbsp **balsamic vinegar**

3 tbsp chopped **parsley**

Salt and pepper

1 Preheat your oven to 200°C (gas mark 6) and slide a roasting tray in to warm up.

2 Bring a pan of water to the boil and when it is boiling vigorously, pour in the lentils and cook them for about 25 minutes, or until totally tender. When cooked, drain the lentils through a sieve and leave to one side.

3 Whilst the lentils are boiling away, tip the broccoli, courgette and radishes into a bowl, pour over the olive oil and season generously with salt and pepper. Carefully pull your preheating tray out of the oven and tip the oil-slicked vegetables on. Place the tray back in the oven and roast the vegetables for 20 minutes, or until they are just tender, but still holding their shape.

•••

4   Add the anchovy fillets, rosemary and chilli to the baking tray and roast the ingredients together for a further 10 minutes.

5   When the vegetables have had their time in the oven, remove them and carefully scrape into a large bowl. Follow the vegetables with the cooked lentils and then balsamic vinegar and parsley. Give the whole lot one final seasoning with salt and pepper before divvying up on to plates and gobbling down.

Courgette and quinoa fritters

Serves **2**
(makes 8)

Cooking time:
30 minutes

These are just great any time of the day and we challenge you not to eat them all as you cook them. They are great dipped hot into a combo of soy sauce and vinegar or at room temperature the next day with a little salad. To ensure these are gluten-free, use tamari.

1 **courgette**, topped, tailed and grated

1 **carrot**, peeled and grated

1 **egg**

65g **feta**, crumbled

100g cooked **quinoa**

4 tbsp **buckwheat flour**

2 tbsp **coconut** or **vegetable oil**

3 tbsp **light soy sauce** or **tamari**

1 tbsp **vinegar** (rice or white wine)

Salt and pepper

1 In a large bowl, mix together the courgette, carrot, egg, feta, quinoa and buckwheat flour along with a pinch of salt and pepper. Mix the ingredients well until they are totally combined and the mix has the consistency of very thick, slightly lumpy double cream – add a splash of water if you need.

2 Heat a little of the oil in a large non-stick frying pan over a medium to high heat. When hot, dollop in mounds of about 1½ tablespoons and flatten them into a rough circle with the back of a spoon – we manage 3–4 in the frying pan at a time. Fry the little fritters for about 4 minutes on each side. They will turn dark golden brown and should be cooked all the way through.

•••

3 When you are happy your fritters are cooked, put them on a piece of kitchen roll to absorb any excess oil. Repeat the process with the remaining oil and fritter mixture.

4 If you've managed to not eat all of your fritters by now, mix together the soy sauce or tamari and vinegar and use as a dip for your fritters. If you have eaten them, then just save the dipping ingredients for another time.

Broccoli and chilli pasta

Serves **1**

Cooking time: **15 minutes**

This is just a very simple, yet classically brilliant flavour combination. The dish really hinges around the humble anchovy, whose flavour is so much more subtle than people presume. They are a great way of making vegetables much more flavoursome. Try this and you'll be hooked.

80g dried **wholemeal spaghetti**

½ head **broccoli**, florets only

2 tbsp **olive oil**

1 **shallot** or ½ **small onion**, peeled and diced

1 clove **garlic**, peeled and finely chopped

3 jarred **anchovies**, drained and chopped into small pieces

1 **red chilli**, de-seeded and finely chopped

1 sprig **rosemary**, leaves only

Salt and pepper

---

1   Bring a large pan of water to the boil and slide in the spaghetti. Cook according to the packet instructions, but 3 minutes from the end, add the broccoli florets to the boiling water.

2   Whilst the spaghetti is cooking, heat the olive oil in a medium frying pan over a medium heat. When hot, add the shallot and garlic and cook very gently for 2 minutes. Add the chopped anchovies and red chilli and continue cooking very gently for another 2 minutes.

3   Chop the rosemary leaves up into small pieces and add those to the frying flavours. Cook the whole lot together for a further 4 minutes, or until the shallot and garlic are soft.

4   Drain the spaghetti and broccoli through a colander. Tip the whole lot straight into the pan with the other ingredients and toss everything together adding salt and pepper too.

5   Pile up your pasta and marvel at the magical flavour from the little fishies.

Fennel slaw with sea bass

Serves **2**

Cooking time:
20 minutes

Fennel has a wonderfully unique flavour and crunch, and one bulb goes a long way. We've paired it up with grilled sea bass, a classic combination. By grilling the bass, you end up with a crispy skin which is filled with all the good fats the flesh doesn't have. If you think bass is expensive, then go down to your local fishmonger and you will soon discover it is not the premium fish supermarkets lead you to think it is.

1 **fennel** bulb, woody outer leaves removed

1 medium **carrot**, peeled and grated

⅛ **red cabbage**, cored and finely sliced

½ **red onion**, peeled and sliced

100g **Greek yoghurt**

1 clove **garlic**, peeled and finely chopped

Juice 1 **lemon**

4 × 100g(ish) **sea bass fillets**, bones removed, skin on

1 tbsp **olive oil**

Salt and pepper

1 Preheat your grill to maximum.

2 Take your fennel and carefully and methodically slice it as thin as possible – don't worry if the bits are all different shapes, just concentrate on trying to make them reasonably thin.

3 Add the fennel to a bowl and follow it with the carrot, cabbage and red onion. Toss the whole lot together until the ingredients are well distributed.

4 In a separate bowl, mix the Greek yoghurt with the peeled garlic, lemon juice and a generous amount of salt and pepper. Scoop the dressing into the bowl of vegetables and toss everything together until thoroughly combined. Leave the slaw to sit for a little bit.

•••

5 Lay a piece of baking parchment or tin foil on a baking tray. Place the fish fillets, skin side up, on the parchment and drizzle with the olive oil. Sprinkle with salt and then slide under your hot grill. Cook the fish for about 8 minutes without turning. The skin should crisp and turn dark golden in places and the flesh should be cooked to bright white perfection.

6 Pile up the slaw and top with the fish fillets for a meal that will make you feel virtuous and healthy with every deliciously crunchy mouthful.

Smoked mackerel and sultana spaghetti

Serves **1**

Cooking time:
20 minutes

Don't you worry your pretty little selves: we here at Student Beans HQ haven't lost our marbles and spiralised our brains to a gooey pulp. This really is a wonderful and traditional Sicilian combo of ingredients. Give it a go and marvel at not only the flavour but also the good fats building up brain matter and the fibre keeping you nice and regular.

30g **sultanas**

80g dried **wholemeal spaghetti**

½ tbsp **coconut** or **vegetable oil**

½ **red onion**, peeled and diced

1 **red chilli**, de-seeded and finely diced

1 large **smoked mackerel fillet**

1 small bunch **parsley**, roughly chopped

1 Tip the sultanas into a bowl and cover with warm water. Leave the sultanas to sit for 10 minutes.

2 Bring a pan of water to the boil and slide in the spaghetti. Cook following the packet instructions. However, just before draining, remove about a quarter of a mug of the cooking liquid and keep to one side.

3 Whilst the pasta is cooking, heat the oil in a frying pan over a medium heat. When hot, scrape in the red onion and chilli and fry for about 4 minutes, or until the onion is soft. Turn the heat off under the pan.

4 Using a knife and fork (to avoid stinky fingers) peel the skin from the mackerel and break up the flesh into small chunks. Add the chunks to the fried onion and chilli, then drain the sultanas and add those too.

...

5 When the pasta is cooked and you have taken your quarter-mug of cooking water, drain the pasta through a colander and tip the cooked spaghetti straight into the pan with the other ingredients. Turn the heat back on underneath the pan, pour in the cooking liquid and toss the whole lot together.

6 When the water has boiled and all ingredients are well-mixed, turn the heat off and stir in the parsley.

7 Pile the pasta high and tuck in. This dish is from Sicily, you now owe us a favour, capiche?

PizzaExpress leggera superfood salad

Serves **2**

Cooking time: **15 minutes**

Containing four portions of vegetables and just 337 calories, the leggera superfood salad screams summer. 'Leggera' means light in Italian and this salad is just that. It's packed with nutritious ingredients including baby spinach, beetroot, avocado, pine kernels, cucumber, lentils, fresh basil and finished with our deliciously creamy PizzaExpress Light House Dressing. We love this salad with the addition of grilled chicken or to up the omega-3 with a salmon fillet.

Seasonal **salad** – any leaves will work with this dish as long as they are fresh and crisp

1 handful **baby spinach** leaves

¼ **cucumber**, sliced

½ **red onion**, chopped

½ **avocado**

1 tsp **tinned lentils**

4 stalks **tenderstem broccoli**, topped, tailed and blanched

1 small ball **light mozzarella**, torn into shreds

1 small **beetroot**, cooked and sliced

1 handful **pine kernels**, toasted

50g **salmon fillet** or ½ small **cooked chicken breast** (optional)

2 pinches chopped **parsley**

8 fresh **basil** leaves

Splash **PizzaExpress Light House Dressing**

1   Place a layer of salad leaves on a large plate, followed by the fresh spinach. Add the cucumber and red onion, along with the avocado.

2   Scatter over the lentils and then layer on the broccoli. Place the light mozzarella on top, followed by the beetroot and a sprinkle of pine kernels.

3   If you want to add the salmon or chicken, do so now, then finish with parsley and basil leaves and a drizzle of PizzaExpress Light House Dressing.

Simple broccoli, almonds and trout

Serves **2**

Cooking time:
20 minutes

Trout is achingly unfashionable. But that's good. It's good because it means the price will always be low for this fish filled with quality fats and a deeper flavour than salmon. Of course, for the unadventurous, you can always revert back to salmon, but give this a go, you might just have found your favourite fish.

250g **tenderstem broccoli**

4 × 125g(ish) **trout fillets**, skin on, bones removed

50g **flaked almonds**

1 tsp **Dijon mustard**

Juice 1 **lemon**

2 tbsp **olive oil**

100g cooked **puy lentils**

1 **shallot** or ¼ **red onion**, peeled and finely chopped

---

1   Bring two pans of water to the boil. Drop the tenderstem broccoli into one and simmer for 2 minutes before draining, then cooling under cold running water. Slide the fish fillets into the second boiling pot, then turn the heat off under the pot, clamp on a lid and leave the fish to bath in the hot water for a minimum of 7 minutes.

2   Toast the flaked almonds in a dry pan for a couple of minutes until they are lightly browned.

3   Mix together the mustard, lemon juice and olive oil in a bowl until the ingredients emulsify to make a dressing.

4   Drop the cooked broccoli into a bowl and add the cooked lentils, shallot and dressing. Toss the whole lot together until you are happy that all of the ingredients are well mixed. Divide the salad between two plates.

•••

5 Carefully remove the fish fillets from the hot water and place on a plate. Using a fork or thick-skinned fingers, peel the skin from the flesh of the fish, then roughly break up the fillets and sit them on top of the dressed salad.

6 Finish your dish with the toasted almonds.

Courgette, poached salmon and pumpkin seeds

Serves **2**

Cooking time:
15 minutes

There is some weird synergy that makes this dish taste far better than its individual parts. Just your normal everyday salad ingredients, but when put together, something really gastronomically special happens. Don't be afraid of poaching salmon, just follow our recipe and you won't go wrong.

---

2 x 150g **salmon fillets**, skin on

40g **pumpkin seeds**

1 small **courgette**, top, tailed and washed

3 tbsp **olive oil**

Juice 1 **lemon**

2 handfuls **rocket**

6 **radishes**, topped, tailed and finely sliced

1 **avocado**, de-stoned

Salt and pepper

---

1 Bring a pan of water to a vigorous boil. Slide the salmon fillets in, place a lid on top and leave to sit in the hot water for 8–10 minutes.

2 Whilst the fish is poaching, pour the pumpkin seeds into a frying pan and toast them over a high heat with a little salt for 2–3 minutes, or until they turn light golden and begin to try and jump out of the frying pan. Tip the seeds on to a plate and leave to cool.

3 Take the courgette and using a decent peeler, peel thin slices of the flesh into a bowl. Do this with a light hand to produce thin ribbons. Pour 2 tbsp of the olive oil in with the courgette ribbons, along with half the lemon juice and a strong pinch of salt and pepper. Mix the ribbons around in their seasoning.

4 Remove the salmon from the hot water with a slotted spoon and drain before placing on a plate. Carefully peel the skin from the flesh using either a fork or courageous fingers.

•••

5 Pile the rocket on to two plates, along with the courgette ribbons and scatter with the radish. Take the avocado and use a spoon to scoop out chunks of the flesh directly on to the salad leaves. Break up the salmon fillets into large chunks and divide equally over your plates. Drizzle the remaining oil and lemon juice over the salad and finish with a scattering of salty and crunchy pumpkin seeds.

6 Whoever you serve this to owes you big time.

Poached salmon and warm bean salad

Serves **2**

Cooking time:
25 minutes

When we think of butter beans, we used to think of our parents' generation, brought up on the unfashionable legume, but how things have changed. They are an excellent low fat source of complex carbs that will keep you feeling full for longer.

½ **red onion**, peeled and finely diced

2 tbsp **vinegar** (sherry, red wine or balsamic)

2 x 175g **salmon fillets**, skin on

1 x 400g tin **butter beans**, drained and rinsed

1 x 410g tin **kidney beans**, drained and rinsed

2 sticks **celery**, topped, tailed and cut into 1cm pieces

1 bunch **parsley**, roughly chopped

½ **red pepper**, de-seeded and cut into 1cm pieces

30g toasted **pumpkin seeds**

2 tbsp **olive oil**

1 Scrape the red onion into a small bowl and pour over the vinegar. Leave the onions to macerate in the vinegar whilst you carry on with the rest of the recipe.

2 Bring a medium saucepan of water to a vigorous boil. Slide the salmon fillets in, place a lid on top of the pan and turn the heat off underneath. Leave the salmon to sit in the hot water for 10 minutes.

3 Whilst the salmon is gently poaching, bring a second pan of water to the boil. Tip both types of bean in and simmer for 1 minute. Drain the beans through a sieve and tip back into the saucepan.

4 Add the celery, parsley, red pepper and toasted pumpkin seeds to the warmed beans along with the macerated red onion and the vinegar from the bowl. Pour over the olive oil.

•••

5 By now your salmon should have had its 10 minutes, so remove from the pan with a slotted spoon, and peel off the skin.

6 Divvy up the bean salad between two plates and top with the perfectly cooked salmon fillets.

Smoked mackerel fried rice

Serves **1**

Cooking time:
12 minutes

Mackerel is brimming with good fats, those essential oils that your body is unable to produce itself so has to rely on you eating. They are the fats that help your body in so many ways, from the production of cells to safeguarding joints from arthritis. Not only is mackerel filled with the good fats, it's also very cheap and easy to get hold of.

½ tbsp **coconut** or **vegetable oil**

3 **spring onions**, topped, tailed and finely sliced

1 small **carrot**, peeled and diced into small pieces

1 clove **garlic**, peeled and roughly chopped

65g frozen **peas**

150g cooked and cooled **brown rice**

1 large handful **baby spinach**

125g **smoked mackerel**, skin removed and flesh roughly broken into large chunks

1 tbsp **light soy sauce** or **tamari**

1   Heat the oil in a large frying pan over a high heat. When hot, add the spring onion and carrot. Fry together for 45 seconds, stirring almost constantly.

2   Throw in the garlic and frozen peas and carry on frying, stirring very regularly for 1 minute, or until you are happy that the frozen peas have defrosted and are virtually warmed through.

3   Tip in the cooked rice and stir together with the other ingredients. Stir-fry the whole lot together until you are satisfied that the rice is heated through. Drop in the baby spinach and stir through the hot rice until it's wilted.

4   Turn the heat off under the pan and gently stir through the flaked mackerel pieces and the soy sauce.

5   Heap up the fried rice and gobble down the goodness.

Kale, mackerel and pomegranate salad

Serves **1**

Cooking time:
15 minutes

Kale – mineral-rich superfood helping to build immune systems everywhere. Mackerel – brimming with essential oils and brain-building fats. Pomegranate – packed with antioxidants and flavour-filled texture. Put the three together in a simple salad, and boom, you'll live forever on a higher plane of intelligence. We've called this recipe gluten-free – just be sure to check the wholegrain mustard for gluten as some brands use a gluten-filled thickening agent.

2 large handfuls **kale**,
  tough stalks removed

1 tsp **wholegrain mustard**

Juice ½ **lemon**

2 tbsp **walnut** or **olive oil**

50g cooked **puy lentils**

1 fillet **smoked mackerel**, skin removed
  and flesh roughly broken up

2 tbsp **pomegranate seeds**

25g **walnuts**, roughly chopped

Salt and pepper

1   Bring a large pan of water to the boil. When boiling vigorously, drop in the kale and simmer for 2 minutes. Drain the kale through a colander and cool straight away under cold running water. Squeeze the kale to remove any excess water and then tip into a large bowl.

2   Make a quick dressing by mixing together the mustard, lemon juice and walnut or olive oil along with a good pinch of salt and pepper.

3   Add the lentils to the kale and pour over the prepared dressing, tossing the leaves in the liquid to ensure they are well covered.

4   Arrange the dressed kale on a plate, place the mackerel pieces on top and finish with a scattering of pomegranate seeds and walnuts.

Nando's chicken meatballs with tomato sauce

Serves **2**

Cooking time: **25 minutes**

This is the flavour from Nando's we all know and love. If you find it too laborious to blitz up your own mixture of thigh and breast, simply use pre-minced breast from the butcher or supermarket.

300g **chicken thighs** (roughly 4 thighs)

1 tbsp **Nando's Peri-Peri Hot Rub**

3 tbsp **plain flour**

2 cloves **garlic**, peeled and grated

2cm **ginger**, peeled and grated

1 bunch **coriander**, finely chopped

2 tbsp **coconut** or **vegetable oil**

1 **onion**, peeled and finely chopped

Splash **red wine**

Splash **red wine vinegar**

1 × 400g tin **chopped tomatoes**

2 tbsp **Nando's Medium Peri-Peri Sauce**

1 Blitz two of the thighs in a food processor until smooth then remove to a bowl. Place the remaining chicken into a food processor and pulse to a rough chop and add that to the same bowl along with the hot rub, 1 tbsp of the flour, half the garlic, the ginger, and half the coriander.

2 With wet hands, form the mixture into 10 balls.

3 Heat 1 tbsp of the oil in a large frying pan over a medium to high heat. When hot, fry the onions and remaining garlic until soft, then add the wine and vinegar and reduce till nearly gone. Pour in the tomatoes and Nando's sauce and simmer for 15 minutes.

4 Heat the remaining oil in a frying pan, roll the chicken balls in the remaining flour and when the oil is hot, brown the balls all over until golden. Then spoon them into the simmering sauce and cook until the chicken is fully cooked through.

5 Add the remaining coriander and serve up.

Restorative chicken noodle miso soup

Serves **2**

Cooking time:
25 minutes

OK, so this soup should sit in every halls of residence behind a 'smash in case of emergency' pane of glass, for those times when you feel a malady sneaking up on you. It is the bastard child of classic chicken noodle soup and miso soup – two of the most comforting soups from around the world both poured into one bowl for your healing.

1 **chicken** or **turkey fillet**, skinless (about 180g)

900ml fresh **chicken stock**

5cm **ginger**, peeled and roughly chopped

40g dried **wholemeal spaghetti**

40g **kale** leaves, woody stalks removed

5 tbsp **white miso paste**

200g **firm tofu**, chopped into 3cm pieces

2 tsp **sesame seed oil**

1 tbsp **light soy sauce** or **tamari**

2 **spring onions**, topped, tailed and finely sliced

1 **red chilli**, de-seeded and finely sliced

1   Bring a pot of water to the boil and slide in your turkey or chicken breast. Let the water come up to a gentle simmer and cook the meat like this for about 8 minutes, or until you are sure it is fully cooked through – you can check by cutting into a thick part of the meat and ensuring the flesh has turned white. Turn off the heat and let the meat sit in the liquid.

2   Pour the chicken stock into a second pan, add the ginger and bring the liquid to the boil. Whilst the stock is heating, take the spaghetti and snap the strands into small pieces straight into the heating liquid. Simmer the spaghetti for about 10 minutes, or until just cooked through.

•••

3 Add the kale leaves and again bring the liquid back up to the boil and simmer for about 3 minutes, or until the kale is just tender.

4 Take the pan off the heat and gradually work the miso paste into the liquid: trying to put it all in at once will result in big lumps of paste bobbing about in your soup – heinous.

5 When you are convinced the miso has been worked in, put the soup back over the heat and when just simmering, add the tofu pieces. Simmer the tofu for about 1 minute, or until you are happy that it has warmed all the way through.

6 Remove the chicken or turkey from the pan and cut it into bite-size pieces.

7 Take the pan off the heat and stir through the sesame seed oil and soy sauce or tamari before ladling the soup into two bowls and finally dressing with the chicken, spring onion and chilli.

8 Sit back, gulp down and feel your body fixing itself with every mouthful.

Turkey and sweetcorn chowder

Serves **4**

Cooking time: **25 minutes**

This recipe is loosely based on the Chinese takeaway classic chicken and sweetcorn soup. We say based, as it isn't brimming with cornflour and preservatives. By whisking in the eggs at the end, your soup will take on a slightly odd appearance, but fear not: as soon as you taste it, you will instantly fall in love with the ugly beauty.

250g **turkey breast**

1 tbsp **coconut** or **vegetable oil**

1 clove **garlic**, peeled and finely chopped

3cm **ginger**, peeled and finely chopped

700ml **chicken stock**

300g **creamed sweetcorn**

3 **eggs**

3 tsp **sesame oil**

3 tbsp **light soy sauce** or **tamari**

2 **spring onions**, topped, tailed and finely sliced

1 Take each slice of turkey breast in turn and slice it into small, thin strips about ½cm thick. No need to obsess about this: a little thin and scraggy is better than thick and chunky.

2 Heat the oil in a saucepan over a medium to high heat. When hot, slide in the turkey, garlic and ginger and fry, stirring almost constantly for 2 minutes – the turkey will probably cook through, but it isn't totally necessary at this point.

3 Pour in the chicken stock and the creamed sweetcorn and bring the liquid to a boil. Simmer the liquid for about 3 minutes or until you are happy the turkey is fully cooked through.

4 Whilst the liquid is boiling, crack the eggs into a bowl and pour in the sesame oil and soy sauce or tamari. Whisk the ingredients together with a fork until fully combined.

...

5 Reduce the heat under the soup just a little and pour the egg in, making sure you stir the soup constantly at the same time. The egg will form small ribbons as it cooks. Bring the liquid up to just under a boil to ensure the egg is cooked through.

6 Serve up the soup in bowls topped with a delicate sprinkling of spring onion.

Chorizo, tomatoes, kale and eggs   page 31

Mushroom freekeh risotto page 112

Salmon and courgette fritters   page 126

Chicken broth page 143–144

Turkey and pork Bolognese   page 157

Chicken bulgur tagine   page 159

World's easiest chocolate mousse   page 195

Spinach satay with turmeric turkey

 Df

Serves **2**

Cooking time: **20 minutes**, plus **1 hour** for marinating

Peanut butter is an economical way to fuel your body with some great fats. If possible try to pick up the unsweetened version, otherwise any virtues of peanut-delivered fat will be totally outstripped by the sugar content.

4 **turkey steaks** (about 100g per steak)

2 tsp **turmeric**

Juice 1 **lemon**

1½ tbsp **vegetable oil**

4 **spring onions**, topped, tailed and cut into 1cm pieces

2 cloves **garlic**, peeled and diced

1 **red chilli**, de-seeded and finely chopped

2 tbsp **unsweetened peanut butter**

4 handfuls **baby spinach**

1 tbsp **light soy sauce** or **tamari**

2 tsp **sesame oil**

Salt

1   Lay the turkey steaks out in a bowl, sprinkle over the turmeric and squeeze over the lemon juice. Drizzle in half the oil and then smoosh the whole lot together until the breasts are brilliantly stained with the turmeric. Leave the steaks to marinade for a minimum of 1 hour or up to 4 hours (too long and the lemon juice will start cooking the turkey).

2   When you are ready to cook, preheat your grill to maximum and lay the turkey steaks on a tray. Season with salt, slide under the grill and cook for 6 minutes on each side or until you are sure the meat is cooked through – you can check this by cutting into a thick part of the steak and ensuring the raw pink flesh has turned white.

3   When you are happy the turkey is cooked through, turn the grill off, shut the door and leave the steaks to rest for a few minutes.

•••

4 Whilst the turkey is cooking, pour the remaining oil into a large frying pan over a medium to high heat. When hot, add the spring onion, garlic and red chilli and stir-fry for 2 minutes. Dollop in the peanut butter and reduce the heat to medium. Add a splash of water and work the peanut butter into the liquid until it has all melted in. Continue to add water, enough to create a thick double cream consistency.

5 Drop in all that lovely baby spinach and work it into the sauce; you might want to whack the heat up a little at this point. When the baby spinach is fully wilted, remove the pan from the heat and pour in the soy sauce or tamari and sesame oil.

6 Serve up the spinach satay topped with yellow turkey steaks.

Body Coach turkey burger with mango salsa

Serves **1**
Cooking time: **15 minutes**

After workouts your body is crying out for carbs, so give it what it needs with this lean turkey burger served on a big white bread bun with a cheeky little salsa. I suggest you serve them with the sweet potato wedges from page 178.

240g **minced turkey**

1 tbsp **fish sauce**

3 **spring onions**, topped, tailed and finely sliced

1 tsp **sesame oil**

½ small bunch **coriander**, roughly chopped

1 **mango**, flesh only, roughly chopped

Juice 1 **lime**

1 small **tomato**, roughly chopped

1 tbsp **reduced fat yoghurt**

1 large **burger bun**

Salt and pepper

1   Preheat your grill to maximum.

2   Plonk the turkey mince into a bowl, season with salt and pepper and add the fish sauce, ⅔ of the spring onion and the sesame oil. Get your hands in and pummel the ingredients together. Working the meat helps it stick together, without any extras like eggs or breadcrumbs.

3   Shape the mix into two thin burgers, place them on a grill tray and slide under the grill. Cook for 6 minutes on each side or until you are happy that they are fully cooked through.

4   Whilst the burgers are cooking, mix together the remaining spring onion, the coriander, mango pieces, lime juice and tomato along with a good pinch of salt.

5   Spread the yoghurt on to the burger bun and when you are happy the burgers are cooked through, pile them into the bun, top with the salsa and stick the lid on.

6   This is a proper double-hander.

Korean pork and rice bowl

Serves **2**

Cooking time:
30 minutes, plus marinating time

Pork loves ginger and chilli like freshers love alcopops and cheap shots. For some reason everybody thinks pork is filled with fat, but it's really not. If you pick up a pork tenderloin, not only is it a cheap source of protein, it is also incredibly lean. To ensure this is free from gluten and dairy, always check the label on the soy sauce.

350g **pork tenderloin**

2cm **ginger**, peeled and finely chopped

3 cloves **garlic**, peeled and finely chopped

2 tbsp **light soy sauce** or **tamari**

1 tbsp **coconut** or **vegetable oil**

4 **spring onions**, topped, tailed and finely sliced

1 tsp **chilli flakes**

150g **mushrooms**, roughly chopped into sixths

65g **mangetout** or **green beans**

2 tbsp **water**

2 tsp **sesame oil**

Brown rice, to serve

2 handfuls **baby spinach** or **lettuce**, to serve

1   Cut the tenderloin into strips that are about 1cm thick and about 5cm long. This is not an exact science, but roughly the same size will ensure even cooking. Scrape the prepared meat into a bowl and add the ginger and garlic and then 1 tbsp of soy sauce or tamari. Mix the whole lot together and leave to sit for a minimum of 1 hour, or overnight if you are into planning ahead.

2   When ready to cook, heat the oil in a large frying pan or wok over a high heat. When hot, add the spring onions and stir-fry for 1 minute. Sprinkle in the chilli flakes quickly followed by the mushrooms and stir-fry for 2 minutes.

•••

3 Tip in the marinated pork strips along with all the liquid, ginger and garlic from the bowl and stir-fry for 1 minute. Chuck in the mangetout along with about 2 tbsp of water. Bring the whole lot to the boil and stir-fry for a further 2–3 minutes, or until you are satisfied the pork is totally cooked through – you can check this by cutting into a thick piece and ensuring the raw pink flesh has turned white.

4 When you are happy that the meat is cooked, remove the pan from the heat, stir through the remaining soy sauce or tamari and the sesame oil and serve piled high atop a mound of brown rice.

5 Finish the whole lot with a handful of fresh salad leaves and get stuck in.

Thai pork salad

There are very few cuisines that manage to pack in as much flavour to their salads as that of the Thais. The balance of sweet, sour and salty flavours combines perfectly to dress the crisp leaves and raw vegetables.

400g **pork loin**, cut into 2cm thick strips

1½ tbsp **fish sauce**

2 tsp **honey**

½ tbsp **coconut** or **vegetable oil**

½ **cucumber**, cut in half lengthways, de-seeded and sliced into ½cm moons

2 **baby gem lettuce**, leaves separated

1 **mango**, flesh only, cut into 2cm chunks

75g **baby sweetcorn**, roughly chopped into 2cm pieces

1 small bunch **coriander**, leaves only, roughly torn

1 small bunch **mint**, leaves only, roughly torn

2 tsp **sesame oil**

Juice 2 **limes**

1 Scrape the pork slices into a bowl and pour over 1 tbsp of the fish sauce and the honey. Stir the meat around until you are sure it is well-slicked in the liquids.

2 Heat the oil in a frying pan over a high heat. When hot, add the pork along with any of the juices and stir-fry over the high heat for about 3 minutes, or until you are certain the pork is cooked through – you can check this by cutting into one of the thicker pieces of meat and making sure the raw pink flesh has turned white. When you are happy the pork is cooked, leave it in the pan off the heat.

•••

3   Mix the cucumber, lettuce leaves, mango, baby corn, coriander and mint in a bowl. Mix the last ½ tbsp of fish sauce with the sesame oil and lime juice. Pour the dressing over the salad leaves and lightly toss everything together until well mixed.

4   Pile the salad up on two plates, top with the cooked pork and revel in your new-found favourite salad.

Straight up broccoli and beef stir-fry

Serves **1**
(you really don't
want to share
steak)

Cooking time:
15 minutes

To get the best priced beef these days you should head to a butcher and inquire about cuts like bavette or onglet. They are brilliant bits of steak that are cheap, cheap, cheap and don't lack in either flavour or texture – they're just not that fashionable. If it's not that likely that you'll haul yourself down to the butcher, you can head to the discount aisle towards the end of the day instead and see what cuts are kicking around. This stir-fry can be made with almost any type of beef from silverside to fillet steak. The other option is to just wait for the student loan to come in and have a fillet-fuelled blow-out.

180g **steak** cut into 1cm slices

1½ tbsp **light soy sauce** or **tamari**

1 tbsp **coconut** or **vegetable oil**

3 **spring onions**, topped, tailed and sliced into 1cm pieces

1 clove **garlic**, peeled and finely chopped

½ head **broccoli**, florets only (larger florets sliced in half lengthways)

2 tbsp **water**

30g frozen **peas**

2 tsp **sesame oil**

Brown rice, to serve

---

1 Put the steak slices in a bowl, pour over half the soy sauce or tamari and leave to sit for 5 minutes.

2 After 5 minutes, heat the oil in a large frying pan over a high heat. When hot, chuck in the spring onions and garlic and stir-fry for 45 seconds. Scrape in the beef, along with any of the liquid lurking at the bottom of the bowl and then quickly follow with the broccoli florets. Continue to stir-fry the whole lot together for 1 minute.

3 After 1 minute, pour in about 2 tbsp of water which will steam up immediately and evaporate to almost nothing.

•••

4 Tumble in the frozen peas and stir-fry for 2 more minutes or until you are totally convinced the peas are warmed all the way through. It is not important for the beef to be cooked through; if anything cheaper cuts benefit from speedy cooking.

5 When you are happy the peas are totally hot throughout, remove the frying pan from the heat and stir through the remaining soy sauce or tamari and the sesame oil.

6 Pile the whole lot atop a mound of steaming brown rice and get scoffing before any of your housemates try to 'share' with you.

Wahaca's chipotle meatballs with fresh guacamole

Serves **4**

Cooking time: **30 minutes**

These hearty, warming meatballs are smothered with a delicious smoky chipotle chilli sauce that's a real favourite in Wahaca's kitchens, because it gives a kick to the rich layers of flavour. The meatballs can be made ahead of time and are delicious served inside warmed soft corn tortillas, with a spoonful of fresh cooling guacamole.

For the meatballs:

450g **beef mince**

30g **breadcrumbs**

1 **egg**

1 tsp **oregano**

1 tsp fresh **thyme**

1 small bunch fresh **coriander**, chopped

Salt and pepper

For the smoky tomato sauce:

1 tbsp **olive oil**

1 **onion**, finely chopped

1 clove **garlic**, crushed and finely chopped

½ tsp **cumin**

2 tsp **oregano**

4 tbsp **Wahaca smoky chipotle chilli sauce**

1 × 400g tin **chopped tomatoes**

Juice ½ **lime**

1 small bunch fresh **coriander**, chopped

Salt and pepper

For the guacamole:

1 ripe **avocado**

1 small bunch **coriander**, chopped

½ **red onion**, finely chopped

Juice ½ **lime**

Salt and pepper

For the meatballs:

1 Combine all the ingredients in a large bowl and roll into walnut-sized balls.

2 Fry in a pan until brown on all sides and put aside until required.

...

For the smoky tomato sauce:

1   Heat the olive oil in the frying pan and gently sweat the onion until translucent (around 5 minutes).

2   Add the garlic, cumin and oregano and continue to gently fry for a further 2 minutes.

3   Add the chipotle chilli sauce, tomatoes, salt and pepper, and meatballs to the pan and simmer until the sauce has reduced by 1/3 and the meatballs are cooked through. Finish off with a squeeze of lime juice and the freshly chopped coriander.

For the guacamole:

1   Mash the avocado, coriander and red onion together in a pestle and mortar (or with a fork in a bowl), adding a squeeze of lime and salt and pepper to taste.

2   These meatballs will keep in the fridge for up to 3 days, if reheated thoroughly, and are suitable for freezing.

Dinner

These recipes take a little more time and effort to prepare than those in the lunch section, but fear not, dear studentkind: most of these dishes are conducive to freezing which means that you will always have a tasty, healthy meal to hand. These recipes also work well if you have friends over – just multiply the ingredients . . . or subtract the number of friends you have.

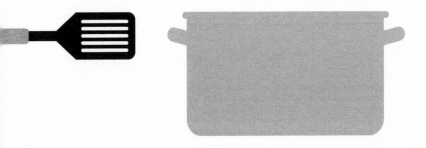

Tomato and dill barley risotto

Serves **4**

Cooking time: **45 minutes**

Dill, you say, not basil? Surely a typo, surely too much matcha tea has gone to our heads? Nope, tomato and basil may be traditional, but they sure aren't exclusive bedfellows. Dill gives this risotto a wonderfully different slant. Oh, and barley instead of rice, that's pretty different too.

1½ tbsp **coconut** or **vegetable oil**
1 **red onion**, peeled and diced
1 bulb **fennel**, topped, tailed and diced
2 cloves **garlic**, peeled and diced
2 sticks **celery**, topped, tailed and diced
1 sprig **thyme**
1 tbsp **tomato purée**

2 large, ripe **tomatoes**, roughly chopped
250g **pearl barley**
800ml–1l **vegetable stock**
Juice ½ **lemon**
1 bunch **dill**, roughly chopped
Salt and pepper

1   Heat the oil in a large saucepan over a medium to high heat. When hot, add the red onion, fennel, garlic, celery and thyme sprig and fry, stirring regularly for 4 minutes. Squeeze in the tomato purée and mix with the other ingredients. Cook the tomato purée for 1 minute.

2   Add the tomatoes to the saucepan along with a splash of the stock. Fry the whole lot together for 2–3 minutes, or until the tomatoes just begin to soften.

3   Pour the pearl barley into the pan quickly followed by 800ml of stock. Bring the liquid to the boil, before reducing to a simmer and cooking for about 35 minutes with a cocked lid. Depending on your tomatoes you may or may not need to add more stock.

4   The risotto is cooked when most of the liquid has been absorbed and the barley is tender. When you are happy that your risotto is finished, remove the pan from the heat and stir through the lemon juice, the dill and a good pinch of salt and pepper.

5   See ya later, basil.

Tomato pilaf

Serves **6**

Cooking time:
40 minutes

This is a foundation dish from which we encourage you to build in different directions, either adding a lump of meat or fish to make this a carnivorous meal, or chucking in some sweet potato and extra veg to keep it meat-free. You might just end up eating it on its own, it's so good.

350g **brown basmati rice**

2 tbsp **coconut** or **vegetable oil**

6 **cloves**

6 **cardamom pods**, bashed with the side of a blunt object

2 **cinnamon sticks**, snapped in half

2 **bay leaves**

2 **red onions**, peeled and diced

5 cloves **garlic**, peeled and roughly diced

5cm **ginger**, peeled and roughly diced

1 tbsp **garam masala**

2 tsp **ground turmeric**

1 × 400g tin of **chopped tomatoes**

300ml **vegetable stock**

1 small bunch **basil**, roughly chopped

1 small bunch **coriander**, roughly chopped

40g **pomegranate seeds**, to serve

1 Tip the rice into a bowl, cover with cold water and leave to soak for 15 minutes. After 15 minutes drain the rice through a sieve and rinse under cold water. Leave the rice in the sieve to drain.

2 Preheat your oven to 190°C (gas mark 5).

3 In a large, ovenproof saucepan heat the oil over a medium to high heat. When hot, add the cloves, cardamom pods, snapped cinnamon sticks and bay leaves. Fry the spices together for 1 minute, stirring almost constantly.

•••

4 Scrape in the red onion, garlic and ginger and cook along with the rest of the ingredients for 5 minutes, or until the onions begin to soften – if you feel like you are burning anything, then just drop the heat a little.

5 Sprinkle in the ground spices and stir into the rest of the ingredients. Keep on frying and stirring for 30 seconds and then chuck in the soaked and drained rice, along with the tin of tomatoes and vegetable stock. Bring the whole lot to the boil. Put the lid on top of the pan (if you don't have a lid then tightly cover with tin foil), slide it into the oven and bake for 18 minutes.

6 When the time's up, remove the pan from the oven and leave to rest with the lid on for 5 minutes. After the rice has rested, take the lid off, fluff the rice with a fork and then sprinkle liberally with the herbs and pomegranate seeds.

Creamy polenta with cumin mushrooms

Serves **2**

Cooking time: **25 minutes**

Polenta is not only a great source of slow-release carbohydrates, but also an incredibly satisfying meal to eat. Try to avoid the quick-cook brands as, although very convenient, they are processed which means you lose much of the goodness from the grain.

500ml **vegetable stock**

125g **polenta**

2 tsp **coconut** or **vegetable oil**

2 tsp **cumin seeds**

250g **mushrooms**, cleaned and roughly chopped into quarters

4 **cherry tomatoes**, cut in half

2 large handfuls **baby spinach**

Juice 1 **lemon**

Salt and pepper

1   Pour the stock into a large saucepan and bring to the boil. Pour the polenta in whilst continuously stirring. Bring the liquid up to the boil and reduce the heat to a simmer, cook the polenta for 2–3 minutes until soft and thick. Season generously with salt and pepper and slide a lid on top.

2   Stir the polenta every two minutes or so whilst preparing your mushroom topping.

3   Heat up the oil in a frying pan over a medium to high heat. When hot, sprinkle in the cumin seeds and let them fry for 30 seconds on their own. Add the mushrooms and let them brown for 2 minutes before chucking in the halved cherry tomatoes and continuing to fry for another minute by which time the tomatoes should start to break down a little.

•••

4 Drop in the spinach and toss with the mushrooms and tomatoes until just wilted. Turn the heat off, season generously with salt and pepper and squeeze in the lemon juice.

5 Serve the mushroom mix on top of piles of steaming polenta.

Kidney bean chilli

Serves **4**

Cooking time:
45 minutes

Chilli à la vegan. Whether you're a bona fide vegan, skint, or have just forgotten to go shopping for a while, it is no bad thing that you are eating a vegetarian meal. Not only does it give your gut a break from working through dense protein, but it also helps the world's climate. Peace, man.

---

1 tbsp **coconut** or **vegetable oil**

2 **red onions**, peeled and roughly diced

3 cloves **garlic**, peeled and roughly chopped

2 sticks **celery**, topped, tailed and roughly diced

1 **red pepper**, de-seeded and roughly diced

1 tbsp **ground cumin**

2 tsp **chilli powder**

1 tbsp **smoked paprika**

2 tbsp **tomato purée**

2 tsp **vinegar** (red wine or balsamic)

1 × 400g tin **chopped tomatoes**

1 × 410g tin **kidney beans**, drained and rinsed

1 × 400g tin **borlotti beans**, drained and rinsed

200ml **vegetable stock**

2 large handfuls **baby spinach**

1 small bunch **coriander**, roughly chopped

---

1 Heat the oil in a large saucepan over a medium to high heat. When hot, add the red onion, garlic, celery and red pepper. Fry the ingredients, stirring regularly for 4–5 minutes, or until the vegetables begin to soften.

2 Sprinkle in the spices, stir into the rest of the cooking ingredients and continue to stir and fry for 30 seconds. Squeeze in the tomato purée, repeating the process of stirring in and cooking out for 30 seconds.

3 Pour in the vinegar which will bubble up and evaporate to almost nothing very quickly. Then add the tomatoes and stir everything together.

...

4 Add both types of bean and the vegetable stock. Simmer the ingredients all together for 15 minutes, by which time the vegetables will be cooked, but should still retain their shape and a slight crunch.

5 Stir in the spinach and coriander, cooking the stew just long enough for the spinach to wilt.

6 Serve up the steaming bean chilli, sit back and think of your contribution to climate control.

Tomato daal

Serves **4**

Cooking time:
1 hour

This daal is brilliant on its own as a warming spiced stew or can be topped with a little roasted chicken or fish to become a more all-round meal. You could also add a carton of coconut milk and blitz it up to make a thick soup. Basically, this is a brilliantly versatile recipe which should be cooked up in big batches and frozen . . . if it lasts that long.

200g **red lentils**

1½ tbsp **coconut** or **sunflower oil**

2 **red onions**, peeled and diced

4 cloves **garlic**, peeled and roughly chopped

5cm **ginger**, peeled and roughly chopped

1 small bunch **coriander**, leaves and stalks separated and chopped

1 **green chilli**

2 **bay leaves**

2 tsp **turmeric**

2 tsp **ground cinnamon**

1 tbsp **garam masala**

5 ripe **tomatoes**, roughly chopped

400ml **vegetable stock**

Salt and pepper

---

1   Tip the lentils into a bowl and either soak in cold water overnight or soak for 30 minutes in warm tap water. When the lentils have had their soaking time, drain them and rinse under cold running water.

2   Heat the oil in a large saucepan over a medium to high heat. When the oil is hot, tip in the red onion and fry for 3–4 minutes, until the onions are just starting to soften. Add the garlic and ginger to the pan and fry along with the onions for a minute. Roughly chop the coriander stalks into 1cm pieces and add to the pan along with the whole green chilli and bay leaves. Fry all the ingredients together, stirring regularly for 2 minutes.

•••

3 Sprinkle in the turmeric, cinnamon and garam masala and fry for 30 seconds, stirring almost continuously so there's no chance of burning the spices.

4 Scrape in the tomatoes and cook them for 2–3 minutes until they start to break down and release their juices.

5 Pour in the stock, add the soaked lentils and bring the whole lot to the boil. Gently simmer the lentils for about 45 minutes, until they are so soft they break up just from stirring. Depending on how vigorously you simmer the lentils and how ripe your tomatoes are, you may have to add a little more water to the pan as you're cooking.

6 When the lentils are totally cooked through, season generously with salt and pepper and finish with the chopped coriander leaves.

Aubergine and sweet potato curry

Serves **4**

Cooking time:
1 hour

On the surface, this looks like just another budget veggie curry to please the students. Well, in some ways it is, but believe us when we say that you will forget any idea of foregoing flavour in return for a few extra pennies in your pocket with your first mouthful.

150g **yellow** or **red lentils**

2 tbsp **coconut** or **vegetable oil**

4 **cloves**

5 **cardamom pods**

2 **cinnamon sticks**, snapped in half

2 **bay leaves**

2 **red onions**, peeled and diced

5 cloves **garlic**, peeled and roughly chopped

5cm **ginger**, peeled and roughly chopped

1 **red chilli**, finely sliced (remove the seeds if you don't like it hot)

1 large **aubergine**, topped, tailed and chopped into 2cm cubes

1½ tbsp **garam masala**

2 tsp **ground turmeric**

1 tbsp **ground coriander**

1 × 400ml can of **coconut milk**

500ml **vegetable stock**

1 large **sweet potato**, peeled and chopped into 2cm chunks

1 large bunch **coriander**, roughly chopped

Juice 2 **limes**

1 Cover the lentils with warm water and leave to bloom for 30 minutes. When they have had their soaking time, drain them through a sieve and leave to one side.

2 Heat the oil in a large saucepan over a medium heat. When hot, add the cloves, cardamom pods, cinnamon sticks and bay leaves and fry for 2 minutes, stirring almost constantly.

•••

3 Crank up the heat a little to medium high and tip in the onions, garlic, ginger, chilli and aubergine pieces. Fry the ingredients all together for 3–4 minutes, or until the red onion is just starting to soften and the aubergine is colouring a little.

4 Sprinkle in the garam masala, turmeric and ground coriander and fry for 1 minute before swiftly following with the coconut milk, stock and the soaked lentils. Bring the whole lot up to the boil before reducing the heat to a gentle simmer. Cook the curry like this for 20 minutes, checking every now and then that it is not cooking dry – if you think it is drying out, then just add a little water.

5 After 20 minutes, drop in the sweet potato, bring back to the boil and simmer for 20 minutes more, or until the sweet potato and lentils are both tender. Again, keep half an eye on the level of liquid.

6 Finish your curry with freshly chopped coriander and the lime juice.

Mushroom freekeh risotto

Serves **2**

Cooking time:
45 minutes

Getting freekeh with somebody used to mean you wanted to be more than just friends – now however, in the brave new world of ancient grains, it is far more likely to mean that you want to go and buy some wholesome, life-restoring grains with them. If somebody does want to get freekeh with you then have a go with this recipe. Just be sure to pick up cracked freekeh otherwise you will be stirring and simmering for hours. If you don't like freekeh then just use pearl barley.

1 knob **butter**

1 tbsp **vegetable** or **coconut oil**

1 clove **garlic**, peeled and roughly chopped

10 **mushrooms**, brushed clean and roughly cut into small pieces

5 **spring onions**, topped, tailed and finely sliced

250g **cracked freekeh**

1–1.25l **vegetable stock**

75g **mascarpone**

Juice 1 **lemon**

Small bunch **parsley**, roughly chopped

Salt and pepper

1 Heat the butter and oil in a large frying pan over a medium to high heat. When hot, add the garlic, mushrooms and spring onions and stir-fry for about 3 minutes.

2 Pour in the freekeh and stir to mix with the other ingredients.

3 Pour in about a quarter of the stock and as it comes to the boil, stir the mixture. Like a risotto, keep cooking and stirring until most of the liquid has been absorbed then add in the second quarter of liquid. Continue the process until all the stock has been used up and the freekeh is tender – it should take about 35 minutes.

•••

4 Remove the pan from the heat, season with salt and pepper, and stir in the mascarpone until it melts to a creamy sauce-like consistency.

5 Squeeze in the lemon juice and stir through the parsley.

Tortilla pizza

Serves **1**

Cooking time:
25 minutes

So here's the thing: despite all those luscious-looking Italian men and women, pizza really isn't that great for you. The combination of fatty cheese mixed with a ton of refined flour makes for a heady cocktail of ingredients your body doesn't like to eat together. Fear not though, here at Student Beans HQ we have invented our very own version that will fill the void and hopefully help you steer clear of needing a colonic. If you want to bulk up the pizza with a little meat, then just chuck on some cooked ham, chicken or turkey.

50g **kale**, leaves removed from the stalk

½ × 400g tin **chopped tomatoes**

150g tinned **cannellini** or **kidney beans**, drained and rinsed

2 tsp **dried oregano**

1 **red chilli**, de-seeded and finely chopped

1 **wholemeal tortilla**

1 **egg**

Black pepper

---

1   Preheat your oven to 190°C (gas mark 5).

2   Put a pan of water on to boil and when boiling, chuck in the kale and simmer for 2 minutes before draining through a colander and then cooling under cold water. When the leaves are cool enough for you to handle, pick them up and squeeze as much of the excess liquid out as possible.

3   Throw the blanched and squeezed kale into a bowl and pour in the tomatoes, beans, oregano and chilli along with a good grind of black pepper.

•••

4 Lay the tortilla on to a flat baking tray and carefully spoon the bean and tomato mixture on top. Slide the tray into your hot oven and bake for 7 minutes.

5 Carefully remove the pizza from the oven, and push some of the sauce from the centre to make a subtle well. Crack the egg into the well and slide the pizza back into the oven to cook for a further 7–8 minutes or until the egg white is set, but the yolk still runs.

6 Remove the pizza from the oven, slide on to a plate and cut up and eat just like momma used to.

Butternut and tomato stew with leek and feta crumble

Here's a budget-beating tasty dinner party meal that will keep your innards as happy as your bank account.

Serves **4**

Cooking time:
1 hour

3 tbsp **coconut** or **vegetable oil**

2 **red onions**, peeled and diced

1 **red pepper**, de-seeded and finely sliced

1 **butternut squash**, peeled and chopped into 2cm chunks (roughly 700g)

1 **carrot**, peeled and cut into 2cm chunks

8 **sage** leaves, roughly chopped

2 sprigs **thyme**

2 tbsp **tomato purée**

1 x 400g tin **chopped tomatoes**

200ml **vegetable stock**

50g **yellow lentils**

1 **leek**, washed, topped, tailed and roughly chopped into 1cm pieces

75g **ground almonds**

75g gluten-free **rolled oats**

75g **pumpkin seeds**

75g **feta**

Side **salad**, to serve

1 Preheat your oven to 190°C (gas mark 5)

2 Heat half of the oil in a large saucepan over a medium to high heat. When hot, chuck in the red onion and red pepper and fry, stirring regularly for 3 minutes, or until the vegetables are just starting to soften.

3 Add the butternut squash, carrot, sage and thyme and continue cooking and stirring for a further 3–4 minutes. Squeeze in the tomato purée and mix in with the other ingredients and just keep on stirring and frying for another minute.

•••

4 Pour in the tomatoes and vegetable stock and bring the whole lot to the boil. Sprinkle in the lentils, give everything a stir and leave to simmer for 45 minutes, or until the squash and the lentils are just tender. Tip the filling into a pie dish.

5 Whilst the filling is bubbling away, heat the remaining oil in a frying pan over a medium heat and add the leek. Fry the leek, stirring regularly for about 2 minutes, or until totally soft. Turn the heat off and stir in the ground almonds, rolled oats and pumpkin seeds. The ingredients should absorb the moisture and become quite dry.

6 Sprinkle the leek mix over the top of the filling (there is no neat way to do this), crumble over the feta and slide the dish into the oven. Bake for 20 minutes, or until the feta is starting to melt and turn golden and the filling is bubbling up the sides.

7 Serve up the pie with a big side salad and an even bigger grin.

Aubergine, paneer and chickpea curry

Serves **2**

Cooking time:
15 minutes

Paneer is the less salty cousin of halloumi. On its own it tastes pretty bland, but like many mild-flavoured foods, it becomes a perfect conduit for curry flavours. Throw in a bit of aubergine, some peas and spinach and you have yourself a very quick, tasty and nutritious meal. If you want to bulk this out a little, then just serve with some brown rice.

If you are a coeliac, pregnant, have a nut allergy or have a compromised immune system for any other reason, please consult the packaging.

---

1 tbsp **coconut** or **vegetable oil**

1 **red onion**, peeled and diced

2 cloves **garlic**, peeled and roughly diced

2cm **ginger**, peeled and roughly chopped

1 small **aubergine**, topped, tailed and cut into 2cm cubes

100g **paneer**, cut into 2cm cubes

1½ tbsp **garam masala**

2 tsp **ground cinnamon**

1 tbsp **tomato purée**

2 **tomatoes**, roughly chopped

100ml **water**

1 x 400g tin **chickpeas**, drained and rinsed

1 small bunch **coriander**, roughly chopped

---

1 Heat the coconut oil in a large frying pan over a medium to high heat. When melted and hot, add the red onion and fry for 1 minute. Chuck in the garlic, ginger and aubergine and continue to stir-fry for 3 minutes or until the aubergine has taken on a little colour.

2 Add the paneer along with the garam masala and cinnamon, and stir-fry for a further 30 seconds before adding the tomato purée and stirring in with the rest of the ingredients.

•••

3 Scrape in the tomatoes along with about 100ml of water and stir whilst bringing the liquid up to the boil. Simmer the ingredients for 10 minutes, or until the aubergine is soft.

4 Tumble in the chickpeas and bring the whole lot back up to the boil. Simmer until you are happy the chickpeas are warmed through.

5 Remove the pan from the heat and add the coriander.

Budget beating burger

Serves **2**
(makes
4 patties)

Cooking time:
40 minutes

This is, in any other terms, a veggie burger. But unlike many such burgers it does not try to replicate meat, but instead stands proudly on its own. If you're not into gluten then just ditch the burger bun and give yourself an extra burger instead.

300g tinned **kidney beans**, drained and rinsed

1 **carrot**, peeled and grated

5 **spring onions**, topped, tailed and finely sliced

1 large raw **beetroot**, peeled and grated

1 **egg**

1 tsp **ground cumin**

1 tsp **smoked paprika**

2 tbsp **coconut** or **vegetable oil**

Greek yoghurt, to serve

4 small, **wholemeal bread rolls**, to serve

Lettuce, to serve

1 large **tomato**, sliced

Sliced **gherkin**, to serve (optional, but you should)

Salt and pepper

1   Bring a pan of water to the boil and drop in the kidney beans. Boil the beans for about 8 minutes by which time they should be really soft. Drain them through a sieve.

2   Tip the beans into a bowl and mush them up with a potato masher. Add the carrot, spring onion, beetroot, egg, cumin, paprika and a generous pinch of salt and pepper. Get your hands in and knead the whole lot together.

•••

3 Heat the oil in a large frying pan over a medium to high heat. Use slightly damp hands to form 4 patties of roughly equal size and thickness. When the oil is hot, gently lay the burgers in and fry them for 3–4 minutes each side, or until nicely browned and warmed through.

4 Build up your burgers by spreading yoghurt on the buns, placing the cooked patties on top and then garnishing with lettuce, tomato and gherkin or your favourite burger toppings.

YO! Sushi's okonomiyaki

Serves **2**
(makes 2 ×
30cm pancakes)

Cooking time:
40 minutes

Okonomiyaki is a Japanese savoury pancake from Osaka. The name is derived from the word okonomi, meaning 'what you like' or 'what you want', and yaki meaning 'grilled' or 'cooked'. It's a popular main dish as people can choose what they'd like in it, perfect to make with leftovers. Our recipe contains prawns, bacon and bonito flakes, but if you'd prefer a vegetarian option then replace these with peppers or mushrooms. These ingredients are available in most large supermarkets or Japanese/Asian stores.

150g **plain flour**

150ml **water**

1 tsp **baking powder**

1 tsp **salt**

2 **eggs**

2 large handfuls **cabbage**, shredded

75g **beansprouts**

60g cooked **small prawns**

75g fried **bacon** cubes

3 tbsp **vegetable oil**

75g ready-to-wok **udon noodles**

Mayonnaise, to serve

Tonkatsu sauce, to serve

Bonito flakes, to serve

1   In a large bowl, whisk together the plain flour, water, baking powder, salt and the eggs until smooth.

2   Oil a griddle or large non-stick frying pan over a high heat and pour in half the batter to make a pancake around 30cm across.

3   Add half the cabbage, beansprouts, prawns (and any other ingredients) to the top of the pancake, adding the bacon bits last.

4   After the cabbage has cooked down and compressed a bit, flip over the whole stack.

•••

5 Stir-fry half the noodles in a little vegetable oil over a high heat in a second frying pan.

6 When the okonomiyaki is cooked, slide it on top of the noodles and garnish with mayonnaise, tonkatsu sauce and bonito flakes. Slide the whole lot on to a plate.

7 Repeat the process with the remaining batter and ingredients.

Baked mushrooms with bulgur and tinned sardines

Serves **2**

Cooking time:
50 minutes

Yes, tinned sardines, get over it. You want quality protein teeming with good fats on a budget? Well then, you're going to have to eat some tinned fish. We think tinned sardines are awesome – let those foodie snobs go choke on their foie gras and turbot terrine. This is as tasty eaten at room temperature as it is piping hot from the oven so it makes it perfect for a campus pack-up.

250ml **vegetable stock**

60g **bulgur wheat**

4 **portobello mushrooms**

2 tbsp **olive oil**

2 large handfuls **baby spinach**

8 **cherry tomatoes**, chopped in half

½ bunch **parsley**, roughly chopped

2 × 120g tins **sardines** in brine, drained

Side **salad**, to serve

Salt and pepper

1   Bring the vegetable stock to the boil. Tip the bulgur wheat into a large bowl and pour over the boiling stock. Carefully cover the bowl with clingfilm and leave to sit for 25 minutes.

2   Whilst the bulgur is cooking in the hot liquid, take each mushroom one at a time, pull the stalk from the middle and discard. Place the mushrooms gill side up on a baking tray and drizzle with the olive oil and season with salt and pepper.

3   Preheat your oven to 180° (gas mark 4) and put a kettle on to boil.

4   Tip the spinach into a colander and when the kettle has boiled, pour the hot water over the sitting spinach – the heat should be enough to wilt the spinach. Cool the leaves under cold water and then squeeze them in your hands to remove any excess liquid. Roughly chop the spinach and leave to one side.

...

5 When the bulgur has sat for 25 minutes, remove the clingfilm and fluff the grains with a fork. Add the cherry tomatoes and the wilted spinach to the mix along with the parsley and a decent amount of salt and pepper.

6 Break up the sardine pieces with a fork and chuck those into the mix too, give the whole lot one last toss together and then pile it on to the waiting mushrooms. Don't worry if bits fall to the side; they will become crisp and tasty in their own right.

7 Slide the mushrooms into the oven and bake for 25 minutes or until the mushrooms are just tender. Plate up the mushrooms with a little side salad and a final sprinkle of salt and pepper. Tinned food never tasted so good.

Salmon and courgette fritters

Serves **4**
(makes
about 12)

Cooking time:
20 minutes

These little beauties came to us at the end of a very long day when the cupboards and fridge were almost bare and there was very little will to cook anything. This soon changed when we started frying these bad boys up and ended up eating them straight from the pan. We're just guessing the soy sauce/tamari and vinegar dip works, because none of our fritters ever made it that far.

1 × 212g tin **pink salmon**

1 small **courgette**, topped, tailed
  and grated

75g cooked **quinoa**

50g **feta**, crumbled

1 **egg**

Vegetable or **coconut oil**
  for frying

3 tbsp **light soy sauce** or **tamari**

1 tbsp **rice vinegar**

1   Drain the salmon of any brine or oil and then fork it into a bowl, breaking up the flesh into small pieces.

2   Pick up the grated courgette, squeeze out any excess moisture over the sink and then add it to the salmon, along with the cooked quinoa and the feta. Crack in the egg and give the whole lot a good mix until it comes together in a rough, loose mix.

3   Heat a little oil in a large non-stick frying pan over a medium to high heat. Pick up small golf ball-sized mounds of the mix in your hands, give them a little squeeze and place them in the hot oil. We manage about 4 mounds in each batch. Use the back of a spatula to flatten the mounds into rounds.

•••

4 Fry the mix for 2–3 minutes on each side or until golden brown. Place the fritters on a piece of kitchen roll to remove any excess oil and then repeat the process with more oil and the remaining mix.

5 Just before serving, mix the soy sauce or tamari and rice vinegar to make a sour, salty dip.

6 Serve up your fritters – presuming you haven't eaten them all straight from the pan.

Fish tacos

Serves **2**

Cooking time:
30 minutes

Not the most convincing title we know, but once you've tried these incredibly simple to make tacos, you'll be extolling their virtues to everybody you know. We've gone with haddock for this recipe, but from salmon to hake, almost any firm-fleshed fish will work.

1 tbsp **dried oregano**

Juice ½ **orange**

3 tsp **smoked paprika**

1 tsp **ground cumin**

1 tbsp **olive oil**

4 × 150g **haddock fillets**

½ **red onion**, peeled and finely chopped

1 **avocado**, peeled and de-stoned

1 small bunch **coriander**

1 **red chilli**, de-seeded and finely diced

Juice 1 **lime**

4 × medium **wholemeal tortilla wraps**

1 large **tomato**, cut into thin slices, to serve

Sour cream, to serve

Salt and pepper

1 Preheat your grill to maximum.

2 Mix together the oregano, orange juice, smoked paprika, cumin and half the olive oil in a bowl. Add the fish and swish it around until you are happy the flesh is all nicely coated. Lay the fish fillets on to a tray and season well with salt and pepper. Slide the fish under the hot grill and cook for 4 minutes before carefully turning and cooking for a further 4 minutes on the other side.

3 Whilst the fish is cooking, tip the red onion into a bowl and scoop the flesh of the avocado roughly on top. Add the coriander, chilli and lime juice along with a generous amount of salt and pepper.

•••

4 Use the back of a fork to smash up the ingredients until they are well mixed. Warm the tortilla wraps in a microwave.

5 When the fish is fully cooked through, remove it from the grill and break up into large chunks.

6 Serve up the fish topped with the smashed avocado, a few slices of fresh tomato and a dollop of sour cream.

Grilled salmon with ratatouille

Serves **4**

Cooking time:
30 minutes

If you think salmon is too expensive, then be brave and head to the fish market to pick up the delicious fish. Make sure to ask for it to be scaled as that really is an awful job. You will soon realise quite how much the supermarkets are charging you for the privilege of packaging and convenience.

---

2 × 175g **salmon fillets**, skin on and scaled

2 tbsp **olive oil**

1 **red onion**, peeled and roughly diced

2 sprigs fresh **thyme**

½ large **aubergine** chopped into 2cm cubes

1 **courgette**, topped, tailed and chopped into 2cm chunks

1½ tbsp **tomato purée**

1 tbsp **balsamic vinegar**

150ml **water**

Salt

---

1 Preheat your grill to maximum.

2 Lay your fish fillets, skin side up on a non-stick flat tray. Drizzle one tablespoon of the oil equally over the fillets and then sprinkle generously with salt. Slide the tray under the grill and cook for 6 minutes. After 6 minutes, the skin should be crisping nicely and even blistering in places; if not, then continue to cook for a little longer. When you are happy, flip the fish over and cook on the flesh side for 4 minutes before turning the grill off, closing the door and letting the fish rest for a couple of minutes.

3 Whilst the fish is cooking, heat the remaining oil in a large frying pan over a medium to high heat. When hot, add the red onion and the sprigs of thyme. Fry the ingredients for 1 minute and then add in the cubed aubergine and the courgette. Crank the heat up to maximum and fry the ingredients together, stirring regularly for 2 minutes.

•••

4 Squeeze in the tomato purée and mix in with the other ingredients, stir-frying for about 30 seconds. Pour in the balsamic vinegar which will bubble up and reduce to almost nothing very quickly. Pour in 150ml of water and bring up to a boil. Reduce the heat to a simmer and cook like this for about 10 minutes, or until the ingredients are just softening. Add more water as you need; don't let the pan cook dry.

5 When you are happy with the ratatouille, when the vegetables are tender, but still holding their shape, divide it up over 4 plates and then top with the perfectly cooked and cooled salmon fillets.

Roast beetroot and red onion with mackerel

Serves **2**

Cooking time: **50 minutes**

Beetroot is not only delicious but it is incredibly good for you. Filled with minerals and fibre, the little purple gems should become a regular on your shopping list. You can, of course, buy beetroot cooked, but for this recipe you need to roast the onions too, so it makes sense to cook the beets from scratch. Just one word of warning: beetroot will stain most of your kitchen utensils as well as your hands. We suggest a pair of Marigolds and lining your chopping board with a little clingfilm or greaseproof paper.

2 medium **beetroots**, topped, tailed and scrubbed clean

2 **red onions**, peeled and cut into 8 wedges each

2 tbsp **olive oil**

4 **mackerel fillets**, skin on

100g cooked **puy lentils**

4 **cherry tomatoes**, sliced in half

2 tbsp **vinegar** (red wine or balsamic)

1 handful **rocket**

Salt and pepper

1 Preheat your oven to 190°C (gas mark 5).

2 Cut your beetroots into 8 wedges each and place them in a bowl along with the red onion. Drizzle with 1½ tbsp olive oil, season with salt and pepper and then scatter the slicked veg on to a roasting tray. Roast the vegetables for about 35 minutes, turning them a couple of times during cooking. You are looking for the vegetables to be tender and slightly coloured around the edges.

...

3 When the vegetables have been cooking for about 25 minutes, preheat your grill to maximum. Line a small tray with baking parchment and lay the mackerel fillets on, skin side up. Drizzle the remaining ½ tbsp of olive oil on top and sprinkle generously with salt. Slide the tray under the grill and cook for 8 minutes without turning. The skin will crisp and turn dark golden in places. Turn the grill off, shut the door and leave the fish in the warm until you are ready to serve.

4 When you're happy the beetroots and onions are cooked, remove them from the oven and leave to cool a little.

5 Tip the lentils into a bowl and add the cherry tomatoes, the vinegar and the rocket along with a little salt and pepper. Scrape the cooked beetroot and onion wedges into the bowl and toss the whole lot together.

6 Divvy up the salad between two plates and then top each one with the deliciously healthy mackerel fillets.

Roast pork tenderloin and pear

Serves **4**

Cooking time: **35 minutes**

Here it is again, that economical, low in fat super-meat: pork tenderloin. This time we've headed back to the orchard and roasted it with delicious pears and then finished the whole lot off with some hazelnuts that are packed with good fats and proteins. This meal has everything. If you're feeling a little naughty and a little flush, then try crumbling some strong blue cheese over the finished dish.

1 **pork tenderloin** (roughly 400g)

½ **butternut squash**, peeled and cut into 2cm chunks

2 tbsp **olive oil**

2 **pears**, cut into quarters lengthways and cored

4 **spring onions**, topped, tailed and cut into thirds

75g cooked **puy lentils**

3 large handfuls **baby spinach** or **salad leaves**

Juice 2 **lemons**

40g **hazelnuts**, roughly chopped

Salt and pepper

1 Preheat your oven to 190°C (gas mark 5).

2 Slice the pork tenderloin roughly into 8 large rounds and place them in a bowl with the butternut squash. Sprinkle with a generous amount of salt and pepper, drizzle with half the olive oil, and toss together to make sure everything is well distributed. Scrape the seasoned ingredients into a roasting tray and slide into the oven. Roast for 15 minutes.

...

3   After 15 minutes, remove the tray from the oven and give the cooking ingredients a little flip around to make sure they cook evenly. Dot the pear quarters and the spring onion around the other ingredients and slide the tray back into the oven. Roast for a further 15 minutes, or until you are certain the pork is cooked through – you can check this by cutting into a thick piece of meat and ensuring the flesh has turned white.

4   Whilst the pork is cooking, tip the cooked lentils into a bowl and add the spinach along with the rest of the olive oil and a decent pinch of salt and pepper. Toss the lot together.

5   When you are happy the pork is cooked through, remove the tray from the oven and tip the lentil and spinach mix into the tray. Toss the cooked ingredients together and then divvy up between four plates.

6   Dress the salads with a drizzle of lemon juice each and a sprinkling of hazelnuts.

Body Coach cheesy beef balls

Serves **1**

Cooking time: **15 minutes**

Juicy balls, bags of flavour and no messing about here. For the little effort that goes into making these, expect maximum flavour. Most supermarkets sell ready-made meatballs (check the label to ensure they're gluten-free), but if you can't find them, then just mix up 250g beef mince with a diced onion and some dried herbs.

1 tbsp **coconut oil**

240g **beef meatballs**

½ **red onion**, peeled and roughly diced

2 tsp **dried oregano**

1 tbsp **Worcestershire sauce**

½ × 400g tin **chopped tomatoes**

30g **cheddar**

¼ **red pepper**, de-seeded and cut into ½cm slices

1 large handful **baby spinach**

Salt and pepper

1 Heat the coconut oil in a large frying pan over a medium to high heat. When hot, chuck in the meatballs and brown all over for about 3 minutes.

2 Whilst the meatballs are browning, place put the rest of the ingredients apart from the spinach in a food processor and blitz until smooth. As soon as the meatballs are browned all over, pour the blended ingredients into the pan, along with a pinch of salt and pepper, and bring up to a boil.

3 Put a lid on top of the pan and simmer for 5 minutes, or until the meatballs are just cooked through – cut into one to make totally sure.

4 Take the lid off and stir through the baby spinach until it has totally wilted into the sauce.

5 Serve up and get lean.

Las Iguanas chilli con carne

Serves **10** generously (perfect for chilli con carne parties, but also great for freezing)

Cooking time: **2½ hours**

The chilli con carne is a stew consisting mainly of beef, chilli, tomatoes and beans and there are many variations out there but we believe ours is the best. It's based on a traditional authentic recipe, using a combination of beef mince and dice for a chunky texture and a perfect blend of fresh and dry spices for amazing depth of flavour. We then finish off our chilli with a combination of seasonings, black turtle beans and freshly picked coriander to give it that truly Mexican feel. We serve ours with garlic and spring onion rice and top it with a choice of spiced butters or soured cream for that fantastic silky finish. A chilli con carne to be proud of!

6 tbsp **vegetable oil**

1kg lean **beef mince**

1kg **diced beef**

2 **white onions**, diced

5 cloves **garlic**, finely chopped

2 **red chillies**, finely chopped, seeds as well

1 tbsp **ground cumin**

1 tbsp **chilli flakes**

¾ tbsp **ground coriander**

¾ tbsp **smoked sweet paprika**

3 tbsp **tomato purée**

6 tbsp **tomato ketchup**

800ml **beef stock**

3 × 400g tins **chopped tomatoes**

1 large bunch fresh **coriander**, roughly chopped

1 tsp **Tabasco**

2 tbsp **Worcestershire sauce**

Juice 1 fresh **lemon**

1 × 400g tinned **black turtle beans** or **red kidney beans** if preferred

Salt and pepper

1 Heat half of the vegetable oil in a large frying pan over a high heat. When hot, add the mince and diced beef and cook until it is well browned. Remove and set aside.

...

2 Turn the heat down to a moderate to low heat, add the remaining vegetable oil to the same pan, and sweat the onion, garlic, and fresh chilli until the onions have softened. Add the dry spices and continue to cook for a further 5 minutes over a low heat.

3 Add the tomato purée and ketchup and continue to cook for a further 5 minutes until a paste is formed.

4 Add the browned beef and mix well with the paste before adding the beef stock and the tomatoes. Bring to a simmer and cover with foil, and cook for 2 hours over a moderate heat.

5 After two hours, add the coriander, Tabasco, Worcestershire sauce, 1 tsp salt, 2 tsp black cracked pepper, lemon juice and black turtle beans. Stir in and cook for a further 5 minutes before serving.

6 Serve with rice, nachos, sour cream, salsa, guacamole, cheese and more Tabasco if you like the extra kick.

Chicken, chickpea and veg stew

Serves **4**

Cooking time:
40 minutes

We would love to say that this recipe was the result of studious testing of flavour combinations and cooking techniques, but it isn't. It's the result of testing a load of recipes and then using all the leftover bits and bobs up in the fridge. We figure it might come in quite useful as we're pretty sure there will be days when all you can find in your fridge are random ingredients that need using up.

2 tbsp **coconut** or **vegetable oil**

6 **chicken thighs**, skinless and boneless, roughly chopped into quarters

1 large **red onion**, peeled and diced

1 (limp) stick of **celery**, diced into 1cm pieces

½ **carrot**, peeled and diced into 1cm pieces

½ **red pepper**, de-seeded and sliced

1 tbsp **tomato purée**

1 tbsp **smoked paprika**

200g tinned **chopped tomatoes**

Juice ½ **orange**

1 × 400g tin of **chickpeas**, drained and rinsed

½ **courgette**, topped, tailed and chopped into 1cm pieces

250ml **chicken stock**

75g **green beans**, topped and tailed

Salt and pepper

1 Heat half of the oil in a large saucepan over a high heat. When hot, add the chicken thighs and brown all over – don't overcrowd the pan, and if necessary brown the meat in two batches using just a splash more oil. When the thighs are golden brown, put them on a plate and carefully tip out any excess liquid from the pan.

2 Pour in the remaining oil and reduce the heat to medium high. Chuck in the red onion, celery, carrot and red pepper and fry for about 3 minutes, or until the vegetables are just beginning to soften. Squeeze in the purée and stir in to the rest of the cooking vegetables. Continue to fry for 1 minute.

•••

3 Stir in the smoked paprika and then swiftly follow with the tomatoes and orange juice, and cook just long enough for the tomatoes to start collapsing. Tumble in the chickpeas and the courgettes and then nestle the chicken thighs back into the mix.

4 Give the whole lot a sprinkle of salt and pepper and then pour over the chicken stock. Bring the liquid to the boil and simmer for 10 minutes, or until you are convinced the chicken thighs are just cooked through – you can check this by cutting into a thick piece of flesh and ensuring it has turned from pink to white.

5 When you are happy the chicken is cooked, add the green beans, bring the whole lot back up to a boil and simmer for 2 minutes, or until the beans are just cooked.

6 Dish out to your friends pretending that you've planned this meal for days.

Chicken in a bag

Serves **1**

Cooking time:
35 minutes

This is probably the healthiest method of cooking chicken you will ever read. No oil, no frying, just gentle poaching in its own juices and a little stock. If you eat this it means you're allowed to eat a chocolate bar and not feel bad about it. To make the meal a bit more substantial, serve with boiled potatoes or wholemeal rice. It is also easily doubled, tripled or quadrupled for a super simple dinner party.

½ **courgette**, cut in half and then into ½ cm thick half moons

½ head **broccoli**, florets only, large ones sliced in half lengthways

3 **spring onions**, topped, tailed and finely sliced

5 **cherry tomatoes**, cut in half

1 **chicken breast**

75ml warm **chicken stock**, from the cube is fine

1 large handful **baby spinach** or **salad**, to serve

Salt and pepper

---

1   Preheat your oven to 210°C (gas mark 6 ½).

2   Roll out a large piece of kitchen foil about 40cm × 20cm and lay it on a baking tray. Pile the vegetables in the middle of the foil. Plonk the chicken breast directly on top of the veg and give the whole lot a generous sprinkle of salt and pepper.

3   Draw up the edges of the foil; they will end up meeting in the middle, but first pull them up to form a wall around the ingredients, so you can pour in the stock without it trying to escape everywhere. Pour the stock over the chicken breast and then draw the sides of the foil in, scrunching them together so the veg and chicken are totally encased.

•••

4 Slide the tray into your preheated oven and bake for 25 minutes.
When the time is up, remove it from the oven and allow the parcel
to sit for 5 minutes before carefully cutting it open (beware of quickly
escaping steam) with a knife and revealing your one-bag dinner.

5 We don't even bother putting the meal on a plate, we just pile
a load of salad on top and get stuck straight in. Bon appétit.

Chicken broth, and what to do with it

Makes **1.5–2l**
depending on
your pan

Cooking time:
**1 hour
45 minutes**

People have been boiling up chicken bones to make soups and stews for centuries. What started as a peasant method of making the most of a chicken has become one of the most ubiquitous and useful food products in the world. From the backstreets of China to the fine-dining kitchens of Paris, everybody makes chicken stock to lengthen sauces, flavour stews and soothe souls.

It is only recently that scientists have started looking at the medicinal properties of chicken stock and have concluded . . . well, they've concluded that aside from high mineral levels, they can't say for sure that chicken broth will make you look younger, cure achy joints, or fix your gut lining as is often claimed. We can only extol the homely and economic virtues of chicken broth and even if it can't be proven to physically help you, we know for sure that chicken broth helps the soul. Amen.

You can use either the leftover carcass from a roast chicken once the meat has been removed, or you can just use a raw chicken carcass, which if you ask nicely butchers will give to you for the small change down the back of your sofa.

---

1 **chicken carcass**, cooked or uncooked – wing bones, thigh bones, leg bones

1 **carrot**, peeled and roughly chopped

1 large **onion**, peeled and chopped in half

1 **leek**, topped, tailed, washed and roughly chopped into 4 pieces

2 sticks **celery**, washed and roughly chopped in half

5cm **ginger**, peeled and roughly chopped into 4 pieces

1 fresh **bay leaf**, 2 if dried

2 sprigs **thyme**

•••

1   Place all the ingredients in a large saucepan and cover with water.

2   Bring the water to the boil, skimming off the frothy scum that rises to the surface. Reduce the heat to a simmer and leave the liquid to potter along for a minimum of 1 hour 30 minutes. The stock can be boiled for up to 2 hours 30 minutes.

3   When the stock has had its cooking time, remove from the heat, leave to cool and then strain through a sieve.

4   The stock can sit in the fridge for up to 3 days. It also freezes very well. Carefully pour the stock into plastic cups and freeze in blocks, then you have portioned stock on standby for anything from soup to stew.

Chicken and vegetable ramen

Serves **1**

Cooking time:
20 minutes

The classic homely dish from Asia that has taken the gastro world by storm is centred on the soup that the noodles and other vegetables sit in. The good news is that once you have cooked up your stock, you will never be far away from a steaming bowl of tasty goodness. We find cooking the ingredients in fresh boiling water and adding the hot stock later works best. This recipe uses soba noodles which are gluten-free (make sure to check the label). If you have no reason to dodge gluten then pick any noodles from udon to egg.

---

1 **egg**

50g gluten-free **soba noodles** (raw weight)

1 head **pak choi**, split in half lengthways

300ml **chicken stock**

1 small handful **baby spinach**

100g **cooked chicken**, roughly chopped or shredded

1½ tbsp **tamari**

2 tsp **sesame oil**

1 **spring onion**, topped, tailed and finely sliced

1 **red chilli**, de-seeded and finely sliced

---

1   Bring a large pan of water to the boil. Carefully lower your egg into the boiling water and simmer for 8 minutes. After 8 minutes, hoik the egg out and run under cold water for 30 seconds.

2   Drop the soba noodles into the still boiling water and cook them according to packet instructions. One minute from the end of the noodle cooking time, add the pak choi to the same pan and simmer away with the noodles.

3   When cooked drain the noodles and pak choi through a sieve and run briefly under cold water to cool slightly.

•••

4 Pour the stock into a saucepan and bring up to the boil.

5 Arrange the baby spinach in the base of a deep bowl. Place the cooked noodles on top and then arrange the shredded chicken and cooked pak choi atop. Drizzle over the light soy sauce and sesame oil.

6 When the stock has boiled, pour it straight over your neatly arranged bowl of goodies. Finish the dish with the spring onion and red chilli.

7 Stick your chopsticks in and slurp away.

Freekeh with spiced chicken thighs

Serves **2**

Cooking time: **45 minutes**

Freekeh, a roasted grain from a mystical planet close to planet quinoa and planet lentil. As you may have guessed, this is another one of those super grains that everybody used to munch on, which was then lost to the mechanical eating of the eighties and nineties and is now making a comeback. It's rammed with complex carbs, fibre and a decent level of protein so is a great alternative to rice and pasta. Although becoming popular, it is not quite so widespread as grains such as quinoa so you might have to look a little further to find it.

---

6 **chicken thighs**, skinless and boneless

3 tbsp **olive oil**

2 tsp **smoked paprika**

2 tsp **ground cumin**

1 **courgette**, washed, topped, tailed and sliced into ½cm rounds

1 **red onion**, peeled and roughly cut into 8 wedges

100g **cracked freekeh**

Juice 1 **lemon**

½ bunch **parsley**, roughly chopped

Salt and pepper

---

1 Preheat your oven to 200°C (gas mark 6).

2 Place the chicken thighs, 2 tbsp of the olive oil, the paprika, cumin, courgette and red onion into a bowl, sprinkle with salt and pepper and toss until you are happy all the ingredients are well distributed. Tip the whole lot into a roasting tray, slide into your oven and bake for 35 minutes, turning the ingredients a couple of times during cooking. This should be enough time to cook the chicken through, but check by slicing into a large piece and ensuring the flesh has turned white.

•••

3   Whilst the chicken and vegetables are roasting, put a pan of water on to heat and when boiling, tip in the freekeh and cook for about 15 minutes, or according to packet instructions (if you haven't bought cracked freekeh it can take a lot longer). When the freekeh is cooked and tender, drain the grains through a sieve and cool a little under cold water.

4   Tip the cooked and drained freekeh into a bowl and add a good pinch of salt and pepper, pour in the remaining olive oil and the lemon juice. Finally, stir through the parsley.

5   Pile the freekeh up on a plate and serve the roasted chicken and veg alongside.

Korean chicken with spinach and brown rice

Serves **2**

Cooking time:
30 minutes
(plus **1 hour**
for marinating)

Korean food has rightly been on the rise over the last few years – it's a truly delicious cuisine that delivers masses of flavour on the back of a few simple ingredients, garlic being one of them. Garlic is not only delicious, but it's also claimed that it can help stave off colds and reduce your blood pressure . . . oh, and it's also good at warding off vampires.

6 **chicken thighs**, boneless and skinless

4 cloves **garlic**, peeled and crushed

3cm **ginger**, peeled and finely chopped/grated

4 tbsp **light soy sauce** or **tamari**

2 handfuls **baby spinach**

2 handfuls **beansprouts**

2 tsp **sesame oil**

2 **spring onions**, topped, tailed and finely sliced

1 tbsp **vinegar** (white wine or rice)

300g cooked **brown rice**

1   Lay the chicken thighs out in a dish and add 3 of the garlic cloves, the ginger and 3 tbsp of the soy sauce or tamari. Massage the ingredients into the chicken meat. Leave the chicken to marinate for at least an hour, or up to 12 hours in the fridge.

2   When ready to cook, preheat your grill to maximum. Line a baking tray with tin foil or baking parchment. Lay the chicken thighs out on the tray making sure they are as flat as possible and that you scrape as much of the marinade on to the flesh as you can.

3   Slide the tray under your hot grill and cook for 6–8 minutes on each side depending on the size of your thighs. To be totally sure the chicken is cooked slice into a thick piece and check that the raw pink flesh has turned white. Turn the grill off, shut the door and leave to rest until you are ready to eat.

...

4   Bring a pot of water to the boil and tip the baby spinach into a colander. Drop the beansprouts in the boiling water and simmer for 30 seconds. Drain the sprouts through the colander with the spinach in – the residual heat will wilt the baby spinach. Run the vegetables under the cold tap to cool then squeeze out the excess water.

5   Place the vegetables in a bowl and add the remaining garlic clove and remaining tablespoon of soy sauce or tamari, as well as the sesame oil. Mix the whole lot together until well combined.

6   Mix the spring onions and vinegar through the warm brown rice then plate up, top with the seasoned vegetables and finish by slicing up the cooked thighs and plonking them (artistically) on top.

Thai turkey balls with soba noodles

Serves **2**

Cooking time:
30 minutes

So you've been on your gap year, you've brought back the sarong, the didgeridoo and some lucky dice game played with the bones of a dead yak, but what you couldn't bring back was the sunshine or that feeling of pure, unadulterated freedom that you left behind on a Thai beach. Well, we're not going to send you on holiday, but if you make these balls and this soup, close your eyes and sit quietly you might go some way to harking back to those carefree travels.
If not your whole body, then at least your taste buds will have fun reminiscing.

100g gluten-free **soba noodles**

75g **green beans**, topped, tailed, and cut into 2cm pieces

500ml **chicken stock**

400g **turkey mince**

1 stalk **lemongrass**, husk removed and the stalk chopped finely

2cm **ginger**, peeled and finely chopped

2 tsp **sesame oil**

1 **red chilli**, finely chopped (take the seeds out if you don't like it hot)

1 small bunch **coriander**, roughly chopped

1 tbsp gluten-free **fish sauce**

2 **limes**

Salt and pepper

---

1 Bring a saucepan of water to the boil and slide in the noodles, cooking them according to the instructions on the packet. A minute before the noodles have had their allotted cooking time, add the green beans and cook in amongst the noodles. Drain the beans and noodles through a sieve and cool completely under cold running water. Leave in the sieve to drain.

2 Pour the chicken stock into a second saucepan and heat gently.

...

3   Plonk the turkey mince into a bowl and add the lemongrass, ginger, sesame oil, red chilli and half of the coriander along with a decent pinch of salt and pepper. Mix the whole lot together using your hands. Knead the ingredients a little to help stretch the proteins, which in turn bind the meat together. Shape the mixture into 12 similar-sized balls.

4   When the stock is simmering, drop in the turkey balls, ensuring they are all immersed in the liquid. You can add a little water if needed, but you should be OK. Bring the liquid back up to the boil and simmer the turkey balls for 7 minutes or until you are happy they are totally cooked through – you can check this by cutting into a large ball and making sure the raw pink flesh has turned white.

5   When you are sure the meatballs are fully cooked through, turn the heat off and add the fish sauce to the stock along with the juice of 1 lime.

6   Divide the noodles and beans between two bowls, pour the hot stock and meatballs over the top and crown with the remaining coriander. Wedge up the second lime and serve with the steaming bowls of memory bliss.

Cornflake katsu

Serves **2**

Cooking time:
45 minutes

Katsu curry should be on the list of highly addictive and dangerous substances. Once you've tried it, you can't stop thinking about the moreish gloop and very soon you are stealing from loved ones to feed your addiction. Stop the process in its tracks by making up this sauce in batches at home. We've gone gluten-free by using gluten-free cornflakes, but you could always stick to traditional cornflakes, or even breadcrumbs.

3 tbsp **coconut** or **vegetable oil**

1 **onion**, peeled and diced

2 sticks **celery**, topped, tailed and finely chopped

2 cloves **garlic**, peeled and finely chopped

4cm **ginger**, peeled and finely chopped

2 **apples**, peeled, cored and grated

1½ tbsp **mild curry powder**

500ml **chicken** or **vegetable stock**

2 **chicken breasts**

1 **egg**

125g gluten-free **cornflakes**

Brown rice, to serve

Salt and pepper

1   Heat 1 tbsp of the oil in a saucepan over a medium heat. When hot, scrape in the onion and celery sticks. Sweat the vegetables together for 6 minutes or until they are beginning to soften, but not colour. Add the garlic, ginger and apple to the mix and continue to fry everything together for a further 5 minutes stirring regularly.

2   After 5 minutes all the vegetables should have softened. Turn up the heat and sprinkle in the curry powder, stirring it in to mix with the other ingredients. Fry everything together, stirring almost constantly for 1 minute and then pour in the stock. Bring the liquid to the boil and then simmer for about 15 minutes, by which time the vegetables

•••

should be completely soft and the stock reduced a little. Using a stick or jug blender blitz the ingredients until smooth.* Leave the sauce to one side.

3   Take each chicken breast in turn and lay it on a piece of clingfilm on top of a chopping board. Lay a second piece of clingfilm on top and then using a rolling pin, saucepan or any other type of blunt instrument, bash the breast until it is about 2cm thick all over. Neatness is not a priority, but even thickness is. Leave the breasts to one side.

4   Crack the egg into a bowl, season with a little pinch of salt and pepper and then whisk until white and yolk are totally combined.

5   Pour the cornflakes into a sandwich bag or carrier bag and with the same implement and vigour with which you attacked the chicken breast, attack the flakes – bash them to smithereens. Tip the 'dealt with' cornflakes into a second bowl.

6   Take each breast in turn and dip into the egg, swooshing it around for total coverage, then place it in the spiky bed of flakes. Push the flakes into the breast until you are happy that the breast is well covered. Repeat the process with the second piece of chicken.

7   Heat the rest of the oil in a non-stick frying pan over a medium to high heat. When hot, gently lay the chicken breasts in and fry for about 3 minutes on each side, or until you are convinced the chicken is fully cooked through – you can check this by slicing into a thick part of the breast and ensuring it has turned from raw pink to cooked white.

8   When you are happy the chicken is cooked, remove it from the pan, blot on a piece of kitchen roll to remove excess oil, then serve up with the brown rice and a generous dousing of the irresistible katsu sauce – addiction never tasted so good.

* If you don't have a blender, then just reduce the sauce a little more and don't worry about the chunks in the sauce: the taste will be just the same.

Turkey koftas with Greek salad

Serves **2**

Cooking time:
25 minutes

Turkey is not just for Christmas. It is without doubt one of the most underused meats on the market and we're not totally sure why. It is a very good source of protein with a very low fat content. Add into the equation the fact it is incredibly cheap and you have a perfect ingredient for health-savvy students.

400g **turkey mince**

2 cloves **garlic**, peeled and crushed

2 tsp **ground cumin**

2 tsp **ground cinnamon**

1 **red chilli**, de-seeded and finely chopped

3 **spring onions**, topped, tailed and finely sliced

¼ **cucumber**, de-seeded and chopped into 2cm chunks

75g **feta**, roughly chopped into cubes

2 ripe **tomatoes**, roughly chopped

Small handful pitted **black olives**

1½ tbsp **olive oil**

1 tbsp **vinegar** (sherry or balsamic)

Salt and pepper

---

1 Preheat your grill to maximum.

2 Tip the turkey mince into a large bowl and add the garlic, cumin, cinnamon, chilli and spring onion along with a generous amount of salt and pepper. Get your hands in and knead the ingredients together until they are well combined.

3 Roughly divide the mix into 6 and taking each portion one at a time, roll it roughly into a ball (wet hands will help the mixture not stick), and then gently flatten and shape into a cylinder shape. Neatness is not paramount here, but try to ensure your koftas all end up about 3–4cm thick. Place the prepared kofta on to your grill tray and repeat the process with the remaining mixture.

•••

4 Slide the tray under your preheated grill and cook for 6–8 minutes on each side, or until you are certain the mixture is fully cooked through – this can be checked by cutting into the thickest part of one of the koftas and ensuring any pink flesh has turned white. When you are happy the turkey is cooked through, turn off the grill, shut the door and leave to rest whilst you make the salad.

5 Tip the cucumber, feta, tomatoes and black olives into a bowl along with a generous pinch of salt and pepper. Pour over the olive oil and vinegar and mix until you are happy all the vegetables are slicked in the oil and vinegar.

6 Pile up the chunky salad and top with the cooked koftas for a tasty, healthy treat that won't break your bank.

Turkey and pork Bolognese

Serves **6**

Cooking time:
**1 hour 15
minutes**

It's a little known fact in this country but a lot of Italians use two types of mince in their Bolognese. Often beef will be joined by pork to add a subtle texture and flavour change to the final dish. We've taken the Italian advice on board and have paired the very lean turkey mince with flavour-filled, slightly fatty pork mince – the combination will not disappoint.

3 tbsp **coconut** or **vegetable oil**

500g **minced pork**

500g **minced turkey**

2 **onions**, peeled and diced

2 **carrots**, peeled and diced

2 sticks **celery**, peeled and diced

3 cloves **garlic**, peeled and diced

2 tbsp **tomato purée**

3 sprigs **thyme**

2 sprigs **rosemary**

2 **bay leaves**

150ml **red wine**

1 × 400g tin of **chopped tomatoes**

500ml **chicken** or **beef stock**

480g dried **wholemeal spaghetti**

1   Heat half of the oil in a large ovenproof dish over a high heat. When hot, crumble in some of the minced pork and fry over the high heat, stirring only a couple of times to brown the meat. Do not overcrowd the pan as this will result in boiling the meat. When the meat is browned, remove it with a slotted spoon and put it in a bowl (to reduce fat even further, drain the meat through a sieve). Brown the rest of the pork and turkey mince using up most of the oil.

2   When all your meat has been carefully browned, drain off any excess liquid, gently wipe the pan clean and put it back on the hob over a medium to high heat. Pour in the remaining oil and add the onions, carrots, celery and garlic, and fry, stirring regularly for about 5 minutes, by which time the onions will have started to soften.

•••

3 Squeeze in the tomato purée quickly followed by the thyme, rosemary and bay leaves. Fry together, stirring almost constantly for 1 minute, then crank up the heat and pour in the red wine. Let the wine bubble up and then reduce to almost nothing. Tip in the tomatoes, rinse out the tin with a splash of the stock and pour that in too along with the remaining stock.

4 Bring the whole lot to the boil and then reduce to a simmer. Cook with a cocked lid, stirring every now and then for about 1 hour, by which time the liquid will have reduced and the meat should be deliciously tender.

5 Bring a pan of water to the boil and slide in the spaghetti, cooking according to packet instructions. Drain through a colander, divvy up into bowls and then ladle over your deliciously rich Bolognese.

Chicken bulgur tagine

Serves **4**

Cooking time: **30 minutes**

The chicken stock plays a far more subtle role in this recipe, being gently absorbed into the bulgur wheat to give it a gentle but satisfying flavour. We like to use bone-in chicken thighs in this recipe, not only for economic reasons, but also to intensify the chicken flavour.

2 tbsp **coconut** or **vegetable oil**

6 **chicken thighs**, skin off

1 **onion**, peeled and diced

2 tbsp **tomato purée**

2 **preserved lemons**, roughly chopped into small pieces

6 **green olives**, roughly chopped

150g **bulgur wheat**

500ml **chicken stock**

1 small bunch **parsley**, leaves only

1 small bunch **mint**, leaves only

50g **feta**, crumbled, to serve

1   Heat half of the oil in a large saucepan over a medium to high heat. When hot, brown the chicken thighs all over. It is likely that you will have to do this in two batches of 3 so you don't overcrowd your pan. The thighs should take about 10 minutes to brown all over. When you have browned the thighs, carefully remove them on to a plate.

2   Drain off any excess fat or liquid in the pan and add the onion. Sweat the onion over a medium heat for about 4 minutes, stirring regularly. The onion should begin to soften and turn translucent.

3   Squeeze in the tomato purée and stir through the sweated onion. Fry the tomato purée for about 30 seconds before adding the preserved lemons and green olives. Pour in the bulgur wheat, stirring it to mix with the other ingredients. Nestle the chicken thighs back into the pan so they all form a single layer.

•••

4 Pour the stock over, it should just about cover the ingredients – if it doesn't then add a little more stock, or even water. Bring the liquid up to the boil, clamp on a lid, reduce to a simmer and leave to cook gently for 20 minutes.

5 After 20 minutes, turn off the heat and leave the stew to sit for 5 minutes. Take the lid off, rough up the bulgur a little and then sprinkle liberally with parsley, mint and crumbled feta.

6 Healthy food has never tasted so comforting.

Chicken and almond tray bake

Here is a classic flavour combination that is easy to cook, and filled with antioxidants and protein. Triple-win.

Serves **4**

Cooking time:
50 minutes

3 medium **sweet potatoes**, scrubbed clean and cut into 6 wedges each

4 tbsp **olive oil**

10 **chicken thighs**, bone-in, skinless

2 **red onions**, peeled and cut into 8 wedges each

4 sprigs fresh **thyme**

2 **red peppers**, de-seeded and cut into 2cm thick slices

12 **cherry tomatoes**

100g **flaked almonds**

2 large handfuls **baby spinach**

Salt and pepper

1 Preheat your oven to 190°C (gas mark 5).

2 Chuck the sweet potato in a bowl and drizzle over half the olive oil along with a good pinch of salt and pepper. Dump the dressed wedges on to a roasting tray ensuring they are in a single layer.

3 Put the chicken into the same bowl and again season with a little salt and pepper. Then arrange the chicken in the same tray as the sweet potato, again trying to keep the ingredients in a single layer (don't worry too much if there's a bit of overlap). Slide the tray into your oven and bake for 15 minutes.

4 Whilst the potatoes and chicken are cooking away, chuck the red onion into a bowl along with the thyme and red peppers. Pour over the remaining olive oil and again season with a little salt and pepper.

•••

5 After 15 minutes have elapsed, take the tray from the oven and scatter the onion mix over the semi-cooked chicken and sweet spuds. Gently toss everything together and slide the tray back into the oven and roast for 20 minutes.

6 After 20 minutes, take the tray out for one last embellishment: tumble the cherry tomatoes and flaked almonds on to the other cooking ingredients, and give the ingredients a very gentle toss. Slide the tray back into the oven and bake for 8 more minutes, or until the tomatoes are just beginning to collapse.

7 Take the tray out, scatter over the baby spinach and toss all together until the spinach has wilted in the residual heat.

8 Serve up to your besties.

Sides & Snacks

This may be a slightly misleading chapter title as many of the following recipes are tasty and fulfilling in their own right. However, they all sit very nicely with many other recipes from the book, or next to a simply grilled piece of meat, fish or tofu. And they'll fill the gap if you want a light munch between meals.

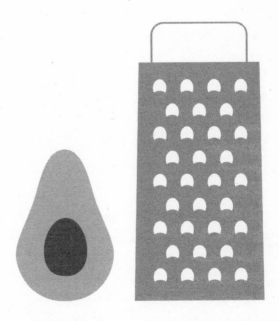

Zingy spiced cauliflower and broccoli rice

Serves **4**

Cooking time:
15 minutes

This is a great little side dish to most meals. It is exactly what it says in the title: broccoli and cauliflower made to resemble (and act) like rice. If you don't have a food processor then don't worry: with a coarse grater, some patience and a bit of elbow grease you can achieve the same result.

---

1 head **broccoli**, florets only

1 small **cauliflower**, florets only

1 tbsp **coconut** or **vegetable oil**

1 tsp **chilli flakes**

1 **lemon**

Salt and pepper

---

1 Put the florets from the broccoli and cauliflower into a food processor. Pulse the ingredients until they resemble coarse couscous.

2 Heat the oil in a large frying pan over a medium to high heat and when hot, add the pulsed florets, chilli flakes and the zest from the lemon.

3 Fry the ingredients, stirring almost constantly for 3–4 minutes or until the vegetables are just cooked through, but are not turning to mush.

4 Season with salt and pepper and, if you like things really zingy, the juice of the lemon. If not, then leave as is and keep the lemon for a swift gin.

Tabbouleh

Serves **4**

Cooking time:
35 minutes

This salad sits as comfortably next to a piece of grilled meat as it does a veggie curry. Satisfying carbs that are rich in fibre seasoned with a bushel of fresh herbs, salty olives and sweet pomegranate seeds – healthy eating doesn't get much better than this.

100g **bulgur wheat**

400ml **vegetable stock**

¼ **cucumber**, de-seeded and cut into 1cm chunks

1 small bunch **mint**, roughly chopped

1 large bunch **parsley**, roughly chopped

Juice 1 **lemon**

2 tbsp **olive oil**

8 **green olives**, roughly chopped into small pieces

100g **pomegranate seeds**

1 Rinse the bulgur wheat under cold running water for 45 seconds and then tip into a large bowl. Put the vegetable stock on to heat and when boiling, pour it over the bulgur wheat. Cover the bowl in clingfilm and leave to sit for 25 minutes.

2 After 25 minutes, remove the clingfilm and fluff up the bulgur with a fork. Add all of the remaining ingredients and mix well with a fork.

Kale and mangetout quinoa

Serves 1

Cooking time:
20 minutes

One pot of boiling water, three different ingredients cooked in boiling water. Now that is efficiency. To make this gluten-free, just use tamari.

100g **quinoa**

60g **kale**, leaves removed from stalk

50g **mangetout**

1 stick **celery**, topped, tailed and cut into ½cm thick pieces

4 **radishes**, sliced in half

1 tbsp **light soy sauce** or **tamari**

2 tsp **sesame oil**

25g **almonds**

---

1   Bring a large pot of water to the boil, then tip in the quinoa and cook according to the instructions on the packet. Around 4 minutes from the end, add the kale, and then 2 minutes from the end, add the mangetout. When the quinoa has had its allotted time, drain through a sieve and cool under cold water.

2   Tip the drained quinoa and vegetables into a bowl and chuck in the rest of the ingredients. Give everything a good mix.

3   Sit back and enjoy the nutty goodness running from your mouth all through your body.

Imam lentils

Serves **4–6**

Cooking time: **50 minutes**

Aubergine is a fine ingredient if you know how to cook it. An excellent vehicle for flavour, it can carry almost any spicing on its gloriously soft flesh. This recipe is a bulked out adaptation of a classic Turkish dish. If you don't mind a bit of gluten in your tummy, then you can use couscous which cooks in less time than the lentils, and to keep it dairy-free just leave out the optional feta.

200g **split lentils**

2 tbsp **coconut** or **vegetable oil**

1 large **red onion**, peeled and roughly sliced

2 **red peppers**, de-seeded and cut into 1cm thick slices

3 cloves **garlic**, peeled and roughly diced

2 medium **aubergines**, topped, tailed and chopped into 2cm chunks

1 tsp **cumin seeds**

1 tbsp **dried oregano**

2 tbsp **tomato purée**

2 tbsp **vinegar** (red wine or balsamic)

1 × 400g tin of **chopped tomatoes**

800ml **vegetable stock**

1 large bunch **coriander**, roughly chopped

150g **feta**, crumbled (optional)

---

1 Pour the lentils into a bowl and cover with warm tap water. Leave the lentils to soak for 20 minutes.

2 Heat the oil in your largest frying pan over a medium to high heat. When hot, add the red onion and peppers and fry for about 3 minutes, stirring regularly. The onion should just begin to soften.

3 Chuck in the garlic and aubergines and fry all together, stirring regularly for 5 minutes.

•••

4 Scatter the cumin and oregano into the pan and follow with a tomato purée chaser. Continue to fry and stir the ingredients for 1 more minute, crank up the heat and pour in the vinegar, which will bubble up and reduce to almost nothing very quickly.

5 Tip in the tomatoes and vegetable stock and bring the whole lot to the boil. Simmer the stew for 10 minutes and then drain the soaking lentils through a sieve and rinse under cold water. Tip the lentils into the pan and simmer the whole lot together for about 30 minutes, or until the lentils and vegetables are all nice and soft.

6 Take your stew off the heat, stir through the coriander and crumble over the feta just before serving.

7 Yet another satisfying method of aubergine prep!

Frijoles

Serves **4**

Cooking time:
40 minutes

This is a wonderful dish all the way from Mexico. Essentially we're just talking about stewed-down black beans with a bit of seasoning and an egg on top, but we firmly believe that this could become the next big breakfast. Black beans contain a wonderfully balanced amount of protein, dietary fibre and slow release carbs, and are sooooooo much more tasty than porridge.

2 tbsp **coconut** or **vegetable oil**

2 **onions**, peeled and diced

1 bunch **coriander**, leaves stripped from the stalk

3 cloves **garlic**, peeled and diced

2 **red chillies**, diced (remove the seeds if you don't like it hot)

2 x 400g tins **black beans**, drained and rinsed

1 x 400g tin **chopped tomatoes**

200ml **vegetable stock**

4 **eggs**

2 **avocados**

2 **spring onions**, topped, tailed and finely sliced

Juice 1 **lime**

Salt and pepper

1   Heat the oil in a medium frying pan over a medium to high heat. When hot, add the onions and fry, stirring regularly for 4 minutes, or until the onions are beginning to soften.

2   Roughly chop the coriander stalks into 1cm pieces and add them to the onions along with the garlic and red chillies. Continue frying the whole lot together for a further 2 minutes.

3   Add the black beans, the tomatoes and the vegetable stock. Give everything a stir and bring it all up to the boil. Simmer the ingredients for 20 minutes, by which time the beans will be very soft and the liquid should have reduced a little to form a thick sauce-like consistency.

•••

4   Using a spoon make 4 little holes in the beans and quickly crack an egg into each one. Let the egg set for 1 minute and then place a lid on top and cook like this for 4 minutes. (If you don't have a lid big enough, then just slide a plate on, or even a second frying pan should sit on top quite nicely).

5   Whilst the eggs are cooking, scoop out the avocado flesh into a bowl, add the spring onions and the lime juice along with a good pinch of both salt and pepper. Mash everything together with the back of a fork.

6   Remove the lid from the pan, scoop out the eggs with portions of the beans and serve with the smashed avocado on the side.

Sweet potato and carrot rosti

Serves **2**

Cooking time:
20 minutes

Sweet potatoes are not only nutritious, they're also conveniently delicious. Although they contain sugar, they are also packed with fibre and complex carbs so your spud high will last and not just spike. This recipe served with spinach and poached eggs is almost as good for your body as it is for your taste buds.

1 **sweet potato**, scrubbed clean

1 **carrot**, peeled

1 **red chilli**, de-seeded and finely sliced

2 **spring onions**, topped, tailed and finely sliced

1½ tbsp **coconut** or **vegetable oil**

4 **eggs**

2 large handfuls **baby spinach**

Sprinkling **chilli flakes**, if you like it hot

Salt and pepper

1 Grate the potato, skin and all, into a bowl. Grate the carrot and add to the bowl too. Pick up the grated vegetables in your hands and squeeze them over the sink – don't go mad, you're just trying to remove a good portion of the liquid to help the rosti be crunchy.

2 Chuck the squeezed vegetables back into the bowl and add the red chilli and spring onions along with a good pinch of salt and pepper and give the whole lot a good toss together.

3 Heat the oil in a large non-stick frying pan over a medium heat. When the oil is hot, scrape the mixture into the pan and use a spatula to spread it evenly over the entire base of the frying pan. Try to make the mix as even all over as possible.

4 Put the kettle on to boil and put a large pan of water on to boil.

...

5 Fry the mix on one side for 6 minutes, checking every now and then that it isn't burning – if it is, just reduce the heat a little. Carefully flip the rosti – we find a combination of two spatulas, or a confident flick of the wrist the best method* – and fry for a further 6 minutes on the second side.

6 Whilst the rosti is cooking, carefully crack the eggs into the large pan of boiling water (for a perfect poached egg, the water should only be just boiling) and poach for about 4 minutes for a soft yolk.

7 Drop the baby spinach into a colander and when the kettle has boiled, pour it over the spinach, which will wilt almost immediately from the heat. Use the back of a spatula to squeeze some of the excess water from the leaves.

8 When you are confident the rosti is cooked, put it on to a clean piece of kitchen roll and dab off any excess oil. Cut the rosti in half and put on to plates. Pile the wilted spinach up on the rosti and finally crown with two poached eggs per plate.

9 Sprinkle with chilli flakes and get stuck in.

* Don't worry if the mix breaks as you turn it, just carefully pat it flat again, nobody will ever know.

Apple and raisin slaw

Serves **4**

Preparation time: **35 minutes** (depending on how speedy you are at chopping)

OK, you've caught us out, this is essentially a Waldorf salad with a couple of other bits thrown in. Well, if you can't beat it then you may as well plagiarise it is our motto. This dish goes perfectly with grilled meats or fish.

---

1 head **fennel**, topped, tailed and finely sliced

3 sticks **celery**, topped, tailed and cut in thin half-moons

¼ **white cabbage**, cored and finely shredded

2 sweet **apples**, cored and roughly cut into thin slices

5 **spring onions**, topped, tailed and finely sliced

50g **pecan nuts**, roughly chopped

65g **raisins**

75ml **Greek yoghurt**

2 tsp **Dijon mustard**

Juice 1 **lemon**

Sprinkle of **cayenne** or **paprika** (optional)

---

1 Scrape all of the vegetables into a bowl along with the pecan nuts and raisins. Toss them together until well mixed.

2 In a second bowl, whisk together the yoghurt, mustard and lemon juice.

3 Tip the dressing over the prepared vegetables and stir in until everything is evenly coated.

4 Plate up the plagiarised coleslaw and finish with an eighties-inspired sprinkling of cayenne pepper.

Tuna avocado boat

Serves **1**

Cooking time:
15 minutes

OK, we can't lie: we haven't invented tuna mayo, but we have made it healthier, adding creaminess with the yolk of a slightly soft egg. Oh, and we've suggested serving it in a boat made from avocado – that's pretty cool.

1 **egg**

1 × 160g tin of **tuna**, in brine, drained

1 **spring onion**, topped, tailed and finely sliced

2 tbsp **Greek yoghurt**

1 **avocado**

Salt and pepper

1 Bring a pan of water to the boil, carefully slide the egg in and set a timer for 8 minutes.

2 In that 8 minutes, fork the tuna flakes from the tin, add the spring onion, Greek yoghurt, a small pinch of salt and a big pinch of pepper. Roughly mix the whole lot together with a fork.

3 Slice your avocado in half lengthways working your way around the stone. Twist the halves to separate them and then scoop the stone out. Use a spoon to work the flesh from the skin in one piece and repeat with the second half of the avocado. Lay the halves on their backs so that the indent is facing you.

4 When the egg has had its 8 minutes, remove it from the hot water and run under cold water until it's cool enough to handle. Carefully peel off the eggshell and then chuck it into the waiting tuna and yoghurt mix.

5 Using the back of a fork, crush the egg and mix it in. The yolk should roughly emulsify into the mix and the white should break up into little flecks amongst the tuna.

6 Dollop as much of the mixture as you can fit in the waiting avocado boats and tuck in.

Super-speedy sage sweet potato wedges

Serves **2**

Cooking time:
14 minutes

The microwave is a much maligned piece of kit, but we think it is an absolute godsend that seems to work on magic. You can obviously roast sweet potatoes in the oven, but these can be made in less than 15 minutes which means you will always have a healthy side dish at your fingertips.

---

2 **sweet potatoes**, scrubbed clean

2–3 tbsp **coconut** or **vegetable oil**

7 **sage** leaves, roughly chopped

Sprinkling **chilli flakes**

Salt

---

1   Prick the potatoes in about 4 places each with a fork and microwave on full power (900w) for 4 minutes, leave to rest for 1 minute and then give them a second blast of 2 minutes, followed by another minute's rest and then one final blast of 1 minute.

2   Take each one in turn and slice it into 4 wedges. Leave the spuds to steam a little whilst you heat up the oil in a frying pan over a medium to high heat.

3   When the oil is hot, carefully place the wedges into the oil and fry for about 2 minutes on each side, or until the flesh is golden brown. Remove the fried potatoes on to a piece of kitchen roll to drain any excess oil.

4   Sprinkle the sage leaves into the recently vacated pan and fry, stirring almost constantly for 2 minutes, then tip on to a piece of kitchen roll too.

5   Plate up the wedges, sprinkle with salt, the fried sage leaves and then finally the chilli flakes.

Chickpea and roast pepper salsa

Serves **2**

Cooking time:
40 minutes

This is a dish that can stand on its own or be paired with almost any cooked meat or fish. Chickpeas are the base of this salsa so you are sure to be taking in a decent amount of protein and fibre. This sort of dish just goes to show how much flavour you can create with only a few simple ingredients.

2 **red peppers**

3 tbsp **olive oil**

1 × 400g tin **chickpeas**, drained and rinsed

1 tsp **dried oregano**

1 tbsp **vinegar** (red wine or balsamic)

½ **red onion**, peeled and diced

¼ **cucumber**, de-seeded and cut into ½cm thick half moons

1 large handful **baby spinach**

75g **feta**

1 small bunch **basil**, leaves only, roughly torn

Salt and pepper

1   Preheat your grill to maximum and take the battery out of your smoke alarm – it might get smoky.

2   Lay the red peppers on a tray lined with tin foil and drizzle over about 2 tbsp of the olive oil. Slide the tray under the grill and cook the peppers for about 15 minutes all together, turning them as the skin begins to blacken – yes honestly, black.

3   When the peppers are fully cooked through and blackened, carefully take them out, plonk them in a bowl and immediately cover with clingfilm. Leave the peppers in their steamy atmosphere for 10 minutes, by which time the skins will have loosened and they should be cool enough to handle.

...

4 When they're ready, take the peppers out of the bowl and lay them on a chopping board. Using a combination of knife and fingers open up the peppers, scrape out the insides and cut off the stem – discard all of this so that you are left only with the cooked flesh. Cut the flesh into long 1cm thick slices and chuck into a large bowl.

5 Add the drained and rinsed chickpeas, the remaining olive oil, dried oregano, vinegar, red onion, cucumber and baby spinach to the bowl along with a generous pinch of salt and pepper. Toss the whole lot together with gentle hands and pile up on to a big plate.

6 Crumble over the feta and garnish with torn basil leaves.

Roast cauliflower hummus

Serves **4–6**

Cooking time:
40 minutes

Here's an all-rounder that can be used straight up as a dip for raw veg, spread across a pitta packed with roast veg or loosened with some warm water to transform it into a sauce for pasta or noodles.

---

1 head **cauliflower**, florets only

4 cloves **garlic**

5 tbsp **olive oil**

1 × 400g can **butter** or **cannellini beans**, drained and rinsed

3 tbsp **peanut butter**

2 tsp **ground cumin**

Juice 2 **lemons**

Salt and pepper

---

1   Preheat your oven to 180°C (gas mark 4).

2   Break the cauliflower florets into a bowl and chuck in the garlic cloves still in their skins, sprinkle with salt and pepper and drizzle with 2 tbsp of the olive oil. Toss the ingredients together and then lay out in a single layer on a baking tray.

3   Slide the tray into the preheated oven and roast for 35 minutes, turning the ingredients a couple of times.

4   Whilst the cauliflower is roasting, bring a pot of water to the boil. Add your chosen beans and simmer for 3 minutes, by which time they should be very tender. Drain the beans and leave them to cool naturally.

5   After 35 minutes, the cauliflower and garlic should both be very tender and golden. Remove them from the oven, carefully tip the cauliflower into a blender and squeeze the flesh of the garlic in too.

•••

6 Add the remaining olive oil, peanut butter, cooked and drained beans, cumin and lemon juice along with a hefty pinch of salt and blend the whole lot up. You might need to add a couple of splashes of water to get the blade moving, but be patient and it will all come together.

7 When cooled, you can store your multipurpose dip in an airtight container in the fridge for up to 4 days.

Mackerel and walnut paté with orange and rocket

Serves **2**

Cooking time: **10 minutes**

There it is again: smoked mackerel, the cheap, cheerful and wonderfully healthy oily fish. This time we've chucked in some more good fats in the shape of walnuts. We've suggested slathering the whole lot on to a crackerbread and serving with orange and rocket, but do not feel wedded to our suggestion: go where your fish-shaped heart leads you.

3 **smoked mackerel fillets**

4 tbsp **crème fraîche**

30g **walnuts**, roughly chopped

4 **crackerbreads**, to serve

1 **orange**

2 small handfuls of **rocket**

Black pepper

1   Take each mackerel fillet in turn and using two forks scrape the flesh from the skin. When you have a chopping board with a load of mackerel flesh on it, keep tearing at it with the forks until it's all in small pieces. Discard the skins and plop the broken-up flesh into a bowl.

2   Add the crème fraiche to the bowl and using a spoon, beat the two ingredients together until you reach a pretty thick, smooth consistency. Drop in the walnuts and give the whole lot one last stir to mix together.

3   Spread the paté evenly over the crackerbreads.

4   Peel the orange and then lay it on its side and cut ½cm thick slices across the circumference of the fruit. Lay the orange on top of the mackerel, top with rocket and a few twists of fresh black pepper and your brain-building snack is complete.

Lean green avocado smoothie

Serves **1**

Preparation time: **5 minutes**

Sometimes you just want your fruit and veg to slip without fuss down your gullet to start healing your body from the excesses that can come with student life. Whether you're trying to make amends for a heavy weekend or you're just feeling like a vitamin boost, this smoothie will sort you out.

1 **avocado**, flesh only

Juice 2 **limes**

250ml **coconut water**

1 **banana**, peeled and roughly chopped

1 tbsp **honey**

1 Put the whole lot into a jug blender and blend until smooth.

Desserts & Treats

You can't be good all the time, but here at Student Beans we can help you to try and be better. Eating healthily is generally about being strong and making choices that override your cravings. However there will be times when you just need that little something sweet to scratch the itch and we hope that the following recipes will go some way to help you avoid an all-out sugar gorge.

Apple and raisin granola bars

Makes
12 squares

These are a great snack to bake up once a week and grab on your way out to lectures. They are the perfect fuel to pick you up out of your 11 a.m. slump: a little unrefined sugar mixed together with the complex carbs of porridge oats will see you through to lunchtime and beyond.

350g gluten-free **rolled oats**
3 **apples**, cored and grated, skin and all (roughly 250g in weight)
100ml **honey**
200ml **almond milk**
65g **raisins**

1 Preheat your oven to 180°C (gas mark 4)

2 Place all of the ingredients into a large bowl and mix until they are all well combined.

3 Tip the mixture into a baking dish (15cm × 15cm) lined with greaseproof paper and slide into the oven. Bake for 15 minutes before removing and leaving to cool.

4 When cool enough to handle, tip the large square out and cut up into satisfying chunks.

Coconut and mango lollies

Makes **12**

Cooking time: **10 minutes**, plus **6 hours** freezing

You may be thinking right now about how expensive mangoes are and how much of a waste of money it is to buy a lolly mould. Well, poo poo to you: for the cost of a couple of shop-bought ice creams, you can make six of these and if you really can't afford the few pounds of investment to buy a lolly mould, then just nab some plastic cups from the dining hall and use those instead.

2 **mangoes**, flesh only

5 tbsp **honey**

Juice 1 **lime**

200g **Greek yoghurt**

300ml **coconut milk**

1   Roughly chop up the mango flesh and place in a blender with the honey and the lime juice. Blitz the ingredients until smooth.

2   Tip in the yoghurt and coconut milk and blitz again until smooth.

3   Carefully pour the mixture into lolly moulds and place in the freezer for a minimum of 6 hours, or preferably overnight.

Choccy-woccy banana boaty-woaty

Serves **2**

Cooking time: **25 minutes**

So if you were ever a cub scout you might recognise this recipe, as it was an oft campfire-cooked pudding to keep the hordes quiet after an afternoon of tent-erecting and playing British Bulldog. What was once campfire fodder now stands proud on the pages of our book as it's actually quite a healthy pudding. The relative healthiness of the dish is directly connected to the cocoa content of your choccy-woccy – anything above 70 per cent and you're civilised and healthy; anything below and you're heading back to the campsite. The choice is yours.

2 **bananas**

About 12 squares of **dark chocolate**

3 tbsp **hazelnuts**, chopped

Greek yoghurt, to serve

1   Preheat your oven to 200°C (gas mark 7).

2   Take a banana and hold it in front of you so it looks like a smile. Gripping one end, cut an incision along the inside bend of the banana, being careful not to slice all the way through. Leave about a 3cm buffer at each end so you don't split the fruit.

3   Gently tease the banana skin open and stuff 6 squares of the dark chocolate into the cavity. Repeat with the other banana and the remaining chocolate.

4   Cut two large pieces of foil about the size of a sheet of A4 paper and wrap each banana up loosely in the foil. Place the bananas on a baking tray and bake in the oven for about 20 minutes, or until you are happy the bananas are soft. (We find the best method of checking is to give them a gentle squeeze with a pair of tongs.)

5   When you are happy the bananas are cooked, remove them from the oven, carefully open up the tin foil, scatter with the hazelnuts and dollop on some Greek yoghurt.

Spelt pancakes

Serves **4**
(makes
about 16)

Cooking time:
25 minutes

Of all the new breeds of old flours, spelt appears to be the most reasonably priced so it makes for a decent fibre-rich alternative to normal plain white flour. It does contain gluten, so maybe you don't see the point in splashing out the extra few pennies, but it might be worth noting that the amount of gluten in spelt is lower than that of normal white flour. Aside from the health benefits, spelt also tastes slightly nutty which makes for a better pancake.

125g **spelt flour**

1½ tsp **baking powder**

1 **egg**

200ml **milk**

Juice ½ **lemon**

Vegetable oil or **coconut oil** for frying

6 tbsp **Greek yoghurt**, to serve

Blueberries, to serve

Honey, to serve

1   Tip the flour into a bowl and sprinkle in the baking powder.

2   Crack the egg into a jug, add the milk and lemon juice and whisk to combine. Pour the wet ingredients into the dry, stirring constantly with a wooden spoon.

3   When all the liquid has been poured in, beat the mixture until you reach a smooth, thick consistency.

4   Heat a small amount of oil in a large non-stick frying pan over a medium to high heat. When hot, spoon in a small amount of the batter (roughly a heaped tablespoon) which will gradually run and form a circle. We can normally fit 4 pancakes in our frying pan at a time. Don't get cocky, just go with what you are comfortable with.

•••

5 Fry the pancakes for about 2 minutes before flipping them. You can tell when they are ready to flip as small bubbles will form at the surface and then hold their shape. When ready, carefully flip the pancakes over with a spatula and continue to cook for about 2 minutes until deep golden brown.

6 Remove the pancakes from the pan and place them on a clean piece of kitchen roll to blot off any excess oil and then repeat the process with more oil and the rest of the batter.

7 Stack the pancakes and serve with Greek yoghurt, blueberries and honey.

Baked spiced apple

Serves **2**

Cooking time:
25 minutes

This is inspired by the classic dish that your gran is probably more familiar with than you are. It takes advantage of the classic Bramley apple which towards the end of summer and beginning of autumn are both cheap and tasty. Normally the apple is stuffed with butter and sugar, but not in this recipe, oh no – we're going for fibre-rich dried fruit and fat-filled nuts.

6 **dates**, pitted and roughly chopped

40g **raisins**

2 **Bramley apples**

30g **ground almonds**

30g gluten-free **rolled oats**

2 tsp **ground cinnamon**

4 tbsp **Greek yoghurt**, to serve

4 tsp **honey**, to serve

1 Preheat your oven to 200°C (gas mark 6).

2 Put a kettle on to boil. Put the dates and raisins into a bowl, pour the boiling water over the dried fruit and leave to stand for 10 minutes.

3 Whilst the fruit is soaking, take each apple and cut in half widthways. Use a combo of teaspoon and knife to remove the core.

4 When the dates and raisins have soaked for 10 minutes, drain about three quarters of the liquid and then chuck the plumped-up fruit into a bowl. Add the almonds, oats and cinnamon and using the back of a fork, crush the ingredients together until they form a thick paste.

5 Use your hands to push some of the paste into the cavity left by the core and then spread the rest over the apple flesh. Place the apples on a tray and slide into the oven. Bake the apples for 20 minutes or until the topping is slightly golden and firm and the apples are tender but still holding their shape.

6 Serve the apples with a good dollop of yoghurt and a drizzle of honey.

World's easiest chocolate mousse

Serves **4**

Preparation time:
15 minutes

We're tempted to just say go buy a chocolate mousse – that would be pretty easy – but alas you would like us less and so would your body. So instead we bring you a non-dairy, non-refined-sugar-sweetened mousse of only three ingredients. Make sure to have some ice in the freezer for this recipe too.

400ml **water**
400g **dark chocolate**, anything over 70 per cent
Handful **hazelnuts**, chopped, to serve

1 Bring 300ml of the water to boil in a small saucepan.

2 Whilst the liquid is heating, break the chocolate into small pieces and place in a medium heatproof bowl. Tip a good handful of ice cubes into a slightly larger bowl and pour in the other 100ml water.

3 When the water is boiling, pour it over the broken dark chocolate and whisk slowly, until the chocolate has totally melted into the water.

4 When you are happy that the chocolate and water are fully incorporated, place the chocolate-filled bowl into the larger one holding the ice and water.

5 Now whisk and slowly but surely, you will feel the chocolate stiffening as you go. Keep whisking until you reach the consistency of chocolate mousse.

6 Spoon the mix into 4 bowls or mugs and sprinkle with hazelnuts. Serve immediately.

Baked fruit with yummy yoghurt

Serves **2**

Cooking time:
20 minutes

We're now going to divulge a little trick that you can use over the course of your cooking career: if you take out fat and sugar from dishes then you will lack flavour, but if you put spices into the mix then suddenly your mind thinks it is eating something sweet. This recipe is a great example of the theory, using ground cinnamon to spike the natural sweetness of the fruit. You can cook this recipe in bulk and keep in the fridge to top yoghurt or porridge with.

2 **pears**, cored and cut into 2cm chunks

2 **plums**, stones removed and flesh cut into 2cm chunks

125g **mixed berries** – we like blackberries and blueberries

1½ tsp **ground cinnamon**

1 **orange**

75g **Greek yoghurt**

2 tsp **vanilla extract**

1   Preheat your oven to 200°C (gas mark 6).

2   Place all the fruit apart from the orange into a bowl. Sprinkle in the cinnamon and grate in the zest of the orange. Gently toss the fruit to try and spread the seasoning evenly.

3   Rip a piece of tin foil about 40cm × 20cm and place it on a baking tray. Pile the fruit up in the middle of the sheet and then squeeze over the juice from half of the orange on top. Draw the sides up over the piled fruit and scrunch them up together to make a parcel.

4   Slide your tray into the preheated oven and bake for 10–12 minutes or until the fruit is just soft (the cooking time depends on how ripe the fruit is – the riper it is, the less time it will take to cook).

5   Whilst the fruit is cooking, mix together the remaining orange juice, the yoghurt and vanilla extract until you have a loose sauce.

6   Pull the fruit from the oven, carefully unravel it, pile up in a bowl and drizzle with the yoghurt.

Blueberry and blackcurrant SuperJam oat slices

These simple bars are similar to flapjacks, but with a gooey layer of SuperJam in the middle!

Makes
8 large slices

Cooking time:
40 minutes

125g **butter**

125g **honey**

250g gluten-free **rolled oats**

½ tsp gluten-free **baking powder**

2 tbsp **blueberry** and **blackcurrant SuperJam** (available from Waitrose or Ocado)

1   Place the butter and honey in a saucepan over a medium to high heat. Heat until the butter has fully melted into the honey.

2   Whilst the butter is melting, tip the oats and baking powder into a large bowl and mix.

3   Pour the melted honey and butter into the oats and carefully mix until all the ingredients are well combined.

4   Grease a small baking tin and line with baking parchment or greaseproof paper, roughly 20cm × 12cm (although you can use a bigger one and just squish the mixture in, it won't spread).

5   Spread half of the mixture across the base of the lined tin and pat down until reasonably even and smooth. Spread the SuperJam over the base then gently top with the remaining oat mixture.

6   Bake the oats for about 25 minutes or until golden brown. Remove the tray from the oven and leave to cool. When cool, chop into 8 slices.

Watermelon pizza

Serves **4**

Preparation time:
10 minutes

This is not so much a recipe as it is a concept. A fun way to make sure you consume a load of fruit. It is a method of fruit service that will make you feel youthful and carefree. We've suggested the ingredients that we like, but from apples to raisins, the fruit bowl is your oyster . . . or something like that.

Juice 1 **orange**
250g **Greek yoghurt**
2 tsp **vanilla extract**
2 tbsp **honey**
1 medium **watermelon**

1 **pineapple**, skinned, cored and cut into 3cm chunks
200g **blueberries**
200g **raspberries**
3 **kiwi fruits**, peeled and cut into ½cm slices

1   Mix together the orange juice, yoghurt, vanilla extract and honey until you end up with a runny, very tasty mixture. Leave the sauce in the fridge until ready to serve.

2   Slice the watermelon into 3cm thick rounds and lay them flat. Give each person a couple of slices and then put all the rest of the fruity ingredients in a bowl. Everybody then decorates their own healthy 'pizza', finishing it all off with a good dollop of the yummy sauce.

3   Mange and feel eight years old again.

Rice pudding with stewed fruit

Serves **4**

Cooking time:
45 minutes

OK, busted: we're using white rice here, so sue us. Actually please don't, instead just enjoy the brief period of white carb liberation. To make up for our heinous crime, we've come up with a totally satisfying pud that isn't brimming with sugar. Instead, by using a combination of spice, almond milk and honey you will soon forget about unnecessary refined sugars and wanting to sue us.

100g **risotto rice**
600ml **almond milk**
2 whole **cardamom pods**, bashed

2 tsp **vanilla extract**
250g **frozen berries** – we like the summer fruit mix
2 tbsp **honey**, plus extra for drizzling

1   Put the rice, almond milk, cardamom pods and vanilla extract into a medium saucepan over a medium high heat and bring to a simmer. Cook gently for about 35 minutes, stirring every now and then until the rice has thickened and is meltingly tender.

2   Whilst the rice is bubbling away, tip the frozen fruit and the honey into a small pan and bring to the boil over a medium heat. Simmer the fruit for about 2 minutes then turn off the heat from underneath and leave to sit until ready to serve.

3   Serve up the rice pudding topped with the stewed berries with an artistic drizzle of honey.

Body Coach virgin piña colada

Serves **1**

Cooking time:
8 minutes

This one's going to take you right back to that beach in Mexico . . . or the local nightclub that does a cheeky offer on piña coladas. No matter where this takes you, it tastes unbelievable. This is a smoothie to be drunk after your workout, as a little snack before your carb-loaded refuel meal.

150ml **pineapple juice**

200ml **coconut water**

4 **mint** leaves

Juice 2 **limes**

75g gluten-free **rolled oats**

1 **banana**, peeled and roughly chopped

1 handful **ice**

1   Place all the ingredients into a jug blender and blitz until smooth.

2   Pour into a glass, stick a tiny umbrella in it and get stuck in.

Super-berry smoothie

Serves **1**

Preparation time: **15 minutes**

No fuss, no bother, nothing weird here: just a classic tasty smoothie packed to the gunnels with vitamins that will make you feel like you can tackle anything. Using frozen fruits not only negates the need for ice cubes, but it is also a far more economical way of buying fruit as there will never be any waste.

40g gluten-free **rolled oats**

300ml **almond milk**

200g **frozen berries** (blackberries, raspberries, blackcurrants)

1 **banana**, peeled and chopped into chunks

2 tbsp **ground almonds**

1 tbsp **honey**

1   Put the oats in a bowl and pour over the almond milk. Leave to sit for 10 minutes until the oats are very soft.

2   Tip the soaked oats into a blender along with the rest of the ingredients and blitz until smooth.

Index

see also smoked mackerel
mangetout: kale and mangetout quinoa 169
    Korean pork and rice bowl 88–9
mangoes: coconut and mango lollies 190
    mango salsa 87
    Thai pork salad 90–1
maple syrup 12
markets 3
meat 3
    see also beef, pork etc
meatballs: Body Coach cheesy beef balls
    136
    Nando's chicken meatballs with
        tomato sauce 80
    Thai turkey balls with soba noodles
        151–2
    turkey koftas with Greek salad 155–6
    Wahaca's chipotle meatballs with fresh
        guacamole 94–5
mint: tabbouleh 168
miso: miso-glazed aubergine and quinoa
    48–9
    restorative chicken noodle miso soup
        81–2
mousse, world's easiest chocolate 195
mushrooms: baked mushrooms with bulgur
        and tinned sardines 124–5
    Body Coach bacon and mushroom
        omelette 28
    creamy polenta with cumin mushrooms
        104–5
    Korean pork and rice bowl 88–9
    ma po tofu 51–2
    mushroom and spinach pasta 41–2
    mushroom freekeh risotto 112–13

N

Nando's chicken meatballs with
    tomato sauce 80
noodles: chicken and vegetable ramen
    145–6
    restorative chicken noodle miso soup
        81–2
    Thai turkey balls with soba noodles
        151–2
    YO! Sushi's okonomiyaki 122–3
nutrition 10–11

O

oats 9, 12
    apple and raisin granola bars 189
    baked spiced apple 194

blueberry and blackcurrant SuperJam oat
    slices 197
Body Coach virgin piña colada 200
granola 17
lassi porridge 18
leek and feta crumble 116–17
overnight oats 22
quinoa power porridge 20
smoothie bowl 19
super-berry smoothie 201
okonomiyaki, YO! Sushi's 122–3
olives: Bill's Israeli couscous salad 43
    Greek salad 155–6
    tabbouleh 168
omega-3 fats 10
omelettes: Body Coach bacon and
    mushroom omelette 28
    prawn omelette 30
    smoked haddock and spinach
        omelette 29
onions: aubergine and sweet potato
    curry 110–11
    butternut and tomato stew 116–17
    chicken and almond tray bake 161–2
    freekeh with spiced chicken thighs
        147–8
    frijoles 172–3
    imam lentils 170–1
    kidney bean chilli 106–7
    Las Iguanas chilli con carne 137–8
    roast beetroot and red onion with
        mackerel 132–3
    superpower salad 45–6
    tomato daal 108–9
    tomato pilaf 102–3
    turkey and pork Bolognese 157–8
oranges: baked fruit with yummy yoghurt
    196
    mackerel and walnut pâté with orange
        and rocket 183
    watermelon pizza 198
overnight oats 22

P

pak choi: chicken and vegetable
    ramen 145–6
pancakes: Body Coach buckwheat protein
    pancakes 23–4
    spelt pancakes 192–3
    YO! Sushi's okonomiyaki 122–3
paneer: aubergine, paneer and
    chickpea curry 118–19

Acknowledgements

This book is the result of a lot of fun, teamwork, support and hard work, all of which we have shared with many people who deserve huge thanks and recognition.

The Healthy Student Cookbook wouldn't be in your hands without the dedication and commitment of our agent Jonathan Conway. Thanks also to the wonderful team at Orion, in particular Amanda Harris for commissioning the book, Tamsin English, our editor, for her patience and expertise, and Helen Ewing for overseeing the thoughtful design.

A huge thanks to the exceptional Student Beans team, especially Ad Taylor, Barrie Smith, Cara House, Charlotte Staunton, Chris Weston, Daniel Eder, Erwin Acosta, Imogen McPhillips, Jamie White, Jay Douglas, Jessica Salvador, Joven Ulip, June Morales, Vincent Siebert, Olivia Newman, Ruth Baney, Seren Altiner, Simon Eder, Stephanie Hanlon, Tiffany Loh, Tom Hargrave, Travis Hall, William Harris and Zack McClelland. Thank you to Jeremy Deaner and Hugh Lloyd-Jukes for supporting us and challenging the status quo.

The unique mix of content would not have come about without the inspiration and outstanding contribution from the most unbelievable group of people and brands. We would like to thank David Deufemia (the greatest personal trainer in London) for working to inspire a healthier way of life and ultimately creating the impetus behind the theme of this book. Thanks to the The Body Coach, Joe Wicks, for his extremely useful input and always finding the time to help out. A huge thanks to Tim Paton, Nicolette Wandrag, David Manly, Robert Gong from Nando's, Imogen Rossi and My Ly from YO! Sushi, Story PR, Rebecca Longhurst and Anneka Dahlhaus from Bill's, Fraser Doherty MBE from SuperJam, Oli Ingham and Paola Feregrino-Rodriguez from Wahaca, Amanda French and Parveen Johal from PizzaExpress, Glenn Evans, Lucy Harwood, Katie Chatterton and Katrina McGrath from Las Iguanas.

Rob Allison would like to thank Hannah, Theo and Tallulah for love and laughter.

Finally a huge thanks to our immediate families. Much love to Stephanie, Toby and Mia for their support and creating a life of joy. Our mum and dad for always being there and supporting our crazy ideas.

Michael and James Eder, founders of *Student Beans*

Also available from Orion

StudentBeans

THE ULTIMATE STUDENT COOKBOOK

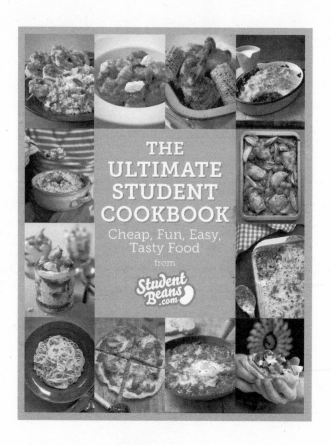